The Dragon and the Cross

The Dragon and the Cross

The Rise and Fall of the
Ku Klux Klan
in Middle America

Richard K. Tucker

Archon Books

1991

© 1991 Richard K. Tucker. All rights reserved.
First published 1991 as an Archon Book, an imprint of
The Shoe String Press, Inc.,
Hamden, Connecticut, 06514

Printed in the United States of America

The paper used in this publication meets
the minimum requirements of American National Standard
for Information Sciences—Permanence of Paper
for Printed Library Materials.
ANSI Z39.48-1984 ∞

Library of Congress Cataloging-in-Publication Data

Tucker, Richard K., 1916–
The dragon and the cross : the rise and fall of the
Ku Klux Klan in middle America / Richard K. Tucker
p.   cm.
Includes bibliographical references and index
1. Ku Klux Klan (1915–   )—Indiana—History.
2. Stephenson, David Curtis, 1891–1966.
3. Ku Klux Klan (1915–   )—Indiana—Biography.   I. Title.
HS2330.K63T84   1991   91-15672   322.4′2′09772—dc20
ISBN 0-208-02310-0

Illustrations appearing in this book are published with permission from the
following sources: Culver Pictures, Inc; Indiana Division, Indiana State Library;
Library of Congress; *Louisville Courier-Journal* (KY); Rutherford B. Hayes Presidential Center, Fremont, OH; Southern Poverty Law Center, Klanwatch, Montgomery, AL; Wide World Photos.

For all the old gang at
The Indianapolis News
where the first ideas for this story began
a long time ago

Contents

Preface

I WAS SEVEN YEARS OLD and half-asleep when I first saw them—strange white figures milling around in an open pasture near a church at the edge of Wever, Iowa. It was late dusk of a hot summer day, and we were returning to the farm in the family Model-T Ford after a long visit to my grandfather's house in Fort Madison.

I remember asking my father: "What are those? Some new kind of animals?"

He laughed. "That's the Ku Klux Klan."

"What are they doing?"

I think he said something about "getting ready to burn a cross." Whatever it was, it meant nothing to me. We didn't stay for the cross-burning. More than two years later, after we moved to Fort Madison, I began to learn more about these mysterious robed and hooded figures, with their flaming crosses on the bluffs overlooking the Mississippi River; and how Catholic children were scared when other kids told them the "Kloo Klux Klan"—as they called it—was "coming to get" them.

But it still didn't make much sense. The Klan came and went in Iowa, "getting" only a politician here and there. In two or three years it was fading away.

Not until many years later, on my first full-time newspaper job—the copy desk of the *Indianapolis News*—did the whole thing begin to come into perspective. A story came across the desk saying that a man named D. C. Stephenson had again been denied parole from Indiana State Prison, where he had already served twelve years of a life sentence for second-degree murder.

After the story moved on to the composing room, in the lull between editions, old-timers on the desk began reminiscing:

Remember when the crowds used to go out to the airfield to see his plane coming in? And how he'd stand up in the open cockpit and wave while the pilot taxied around?

Remember when they'd jam up around the doors to that theater on Illinois Street, when they heard he was at the movies, and wait just to watch him come out? How they'd clap and cheer and yell "Hiya Steve"?

How the hell did he do it?

It was all those hoods and robes and mysterious mumbo-jumbo stuff.

No. It was more than that—a lot more than that.

Off and on for years I wondered: How much "more" of what? How could a so-called Grand Dragon of a now-discredited Ku Klux Klan have enlisted more than a quarter-million of a state's population and taken over its government? How did he use his charisma to build power and reap profits throughout much of the American Middle West?

More recently, I began to dig deeper into what that "more" really was—not only in Indiana but in much of the United States in the middle of the first half of the twentieth century. In the process I began to see a message for our own times, a piece of neglected social history that may be an object lesson for us all.

Acknowledgments

FOR MY FIRST INTEREST in this story I am indebted to many former, senior colleagues at the *Indianapolis News* in those days when their memories of the Ku Klux Klan in Indiana were still fresh. More recently, I have relied heavily on the invaluable services of research librarians. My special thanks go to Laurence Hathaway of the Indiana Division, Indiana State Library, in Indianapolis; Sandra Fitzgerald, chief librarian of the *Indianapolis Star-News*; and Frank Chandler of Evansville's Willard Library; thanks also to the reference departments of the Kokomo-Howard County (IN) Public Library and the Noblesville (IN) Southeastern Public Library. I am also grateful for the assistance of the family of the late John L. Niblack, whose *Life and Times of a Hoosier Judge* provided so much firsthand material for this book, and to Clay Trusty, Jr., for the family memories of the courageous fight his father, the Reverend Clay Trusty, waged against the Klan in Indianapolis. Finally, I must express my appreciation to my typists, Lynn Martz and Sue Nelson, for their patience and efficiency during my numerous additions and revisions.

Introduction: The Realm of the Dragon

It first appealed to the ignorant, the slightly-unbalanced and the venal; but by the time the enlightened elements realized the danger it was already on top of them.—Robert Coughlan, describing the spread of the Ku Klux Klan in Indiana in the 1920s.[1]

HE HAD OFTEN BOASTED, "I am the law in Indiana." He once hoped to become president of the United States. Now, in the first gray light of a November dawn, he sat under guard in a sheriff's car, headed for a life term in the state prison on the shores of Lake Michigan.

The year was 1925. The prisoner was David Curtis Stephenson, a chubby, well-groomed, blond man of thirty-four, erstwhile Grand Dragon of an autonomous Indiana Realm, Knights of the Ku Klux Klan. Until only a few months ago he had been the most powerful man in the state.

His boast had not been an idle one. With more than a quarter-million Klan followers in Indiana alone, and a Klan-based political machine that controlled public offices from sheriff to governor, he had been, in many ways, the law. Beyond Indiana, as the Klan's chief organizer in

1

twenty other northern states, he had built a potent force that he thought might lead him to the White House. He had manipulated a state legislature and grown rich with payoffs from special interests. In the Indianapolis state-house even now sat his hand-picked choice for governor. Only last January the Grand Dragon had been an honored guest at the governor's inaugural banquet in the Indianap-olis Athletic Club.

There he had met and danced with Madge Oberholtzer, a young career woman in the state education department. Dinner dates and political favors followed. But Madge was now dead, and Stephenson was facing a life term for her murder. It had been a shocking affair—a drunken, savage rape that spelled the doom of the Klan in the Middle West. But, until then, Stephenson and his "Invisible Empire" had, in many ways, been "the law."

For more than three years Indiana had been the center-piece, the strongest bastion in the north, of a flag-waving, evangelistic phenomenon that had taken over much of Middle America. While it was called the Ku Klux Klan, while its members wore hoods and burned crosses, it was to its millions of joiners and supporters across America a far cry from the paranoid racist violence so often associated with the robed, redneck fringe calling itself the Klan today.

In Indiana alone up to 300,000 people[2] had joined what they believed to be a crusade for old-time fundamentalist religion, clean living, 100 percent Americanism, and law and order. Invocations of God, flag, and country, more than of white supremacy, spurred its spectacular success.

Mainline Protestant ministers often praised the Klan from their pulpits. Reformers welcomed it to vice-ridden communities to "clean up" things. Prohibitionists and the Anti-Saloon League supported it as a force against the Demon Rum. Most of all, millions saw it as a protection against the Pope of Rome, who, they believed, was threat-ening to "take over America."

The Klan was racist, white, and Anglo-Saxon. It had its violent fringes, mostly in the South and Southwest. But the masses flocking to its flaming crosses, especially in the Middle West, were not out to lynch blacks or to flog adulterers. They were, for the most part, ordinary work-a-day Americans caught up in a rush of flag-waving, nativist nationalism and defensive Protestant-Puritan moral reaction.

In preparation for his definitive 1924 work, *The Ku Klux Klan: A Study of the American Mind,* Dartmouth sociologist John Moffatt Mecklin interviewed hundreds of Klansmen across the country. He found the vast majority to be "conventional Americans, thoroughly human, kind fathers and husbands, hospitable to the stranger, devout in their worship of God, loyal to state and nation, and including in many instances the best citizens of the community."[3]

Their basic problem, he added, was that they were "conspicuously lacking in that refinement of sentiment and critical independence of thought which must be possessed by any individual or group which undertakes to shape public opinion in a democracy." It was not "innate depravity" but "plain old-fashioned ignorance."

The *New York World*'s focus on cases of Klan violence in a widely syndicated 1921 exposé, he said, portrayed the Klan as something alien to American life, and thus missed its "true significance."

"If the Klan were utterly un-American," he wrote, "it could never have succeeded as it did. The Klan is not alien to the American spirit. The Klan is but the recrudescence of forces that already existed in American life."[4]

In a more satirical vein, in a 1923 issue of their *Smart Set* magazine, H. L. Mencken and George Jean Nathan agreed:

> What could be more fatuous than the current denunciations of the so-called Ku Klux Klan as an anti-American organization? It is, in point of fact, probably the most thoroughly American *verein* ever set going in the Republic. It supports the doctrine that obscure and anonymous men have the right to regulate the most private acts and the most private opinions of their betters; it maintains as a funda-

mental principle of law that an unpopular man has no rights in the courts; it resists any and every differentiation of American from American and insists that all shall be identical. . . . All these notions are the heart's blood of Americanism.[5]

Continuing their foray in a subsequent issue, the editors saw the Klan as an inevitable manifestation of Mencken's "Boobus Americanus."

Not a single solitary sound reason has yet been advanced for putting the Ku Klux Klan out of business. If the Klan is against the Jews, so are half the good hotels of the Republic and three-quarters of the good clubs. If the Klan is against the foreign-born or the hyphenated citizen, so is the National Institute of Arts and Letters. If the Klan is against the Negro, so are all of the states south of the Mason-Dixon line. If the Klan is for damnation and persecution, so is the Methodist church. If the Klan is bent upon political control, so are the American Legion and Tammany Hall. If the Klan wears grotesque uniforms, so do the Knights of Pythias and the Mystic Shriners. If the Klan holds its meetings in the dead of night, so do the Elks. If the Klan conducts its business in secret, so do all college Greek letter fraternities and the Department of State. If the Klan holds idiotic parades in the public streets, so do the police, the letter carriers and firemen. If the Klan's officers bear ridiculous names, so do the officers of the Lambs' Club. If the Klan uses the mails for shaking down suckers, so does the Red Cross. If the Klan constitutes itself a censor of private morals, so does the Congress of the United States."[6]

Analyzing the spectacular growth of the 1920s Klan in Indiana, Irving Leibowitz wrote that "Many Klansmen were victims rather than villains. . . . Every responsible source, including those who actively fought the Klan, has agreed that the Invisible Empire was made up largely of people of substantial and decent standing, most of them active members of Protestant churches, with definite if somewhat narrow ideals. Many never knew or understood what the Klan was really like."[7]

4

Another student of the Klan phenomenon, William Peirce Randel, said "the Klan could never have flourished in the United States without the backing of large numbers of people who themselves would never adopt Klan methods. . . . A sober review of our history yields the unwelcome conclusion that the Klan spirit is a constant in our national behavior. At times it is quiescent, but it is not dead; only slumbering between eruptions."[8]

The "constant" Klan spirit that erupted in the early 1920s—the eruption that Stephenson had so adroitly exploited—was a mix of nineteenth century Know-Nothing nativism, provincial Puritanism, and frontier vigilante tradition, fueled by a nationalistic fever left over from World War I. Protestant nativism—antialien, anti-Semitic, most of all anti-Catholic—was the dominant force. One Klan orator spoke for millions when he said: "We want this country ruled by the kind of people who settled it. This is *our* country, and we alone are responsible for its future."[9]

Groundwork for the racialist tribalism that fueled the Klan was laid in the American public schoolbooks of the nineteenth century. In her analysis of many of these books, Ruth Miller Elson found that "each race and its subdivisions—nationalities—are defined by inherent mental and personal characteristics which the child must memorize. . . . The American, as the ideal man, is of the white race, of Northern European background, Protestant, self-made, and, if not a farmer, at least retaining the virtues of his yeoman ancestors."[10]

Blacks took second place to Catholics and Jews as the Klan's targets. In a 1924 pamphlet, the Klan's second Imperial Wizard, Hiram Wesley Evans, wrote: "The Negro is not the menace to Americanism in the same sense that the Jew or the Roman Catholic is a menace. He is not actually hostile to it. He is simply racially incapable of understanding, sharing, or contributing to Americanism."[11]

At its peak, the new Ku Klux Klan of the 1920s—a reincarnation of the original white supremacist group in the Reconstruction South—had an estimated 5 million members nationwide. Far from its southern birthplace, it flourished mightily in such states as Indiana, Ohio, Kansas, and Michigan. Even farther away, it became a force to be reckoned with in Oklahoma, Texas, Oregon, and California.

In the North it was seldom violent, but it wielded formidable and insidious power. Its weapons were social and economic intimidation, boycotts, slanderous propaganda and rumor, awesome spectacles, vigilante patrols, and—above all—the ballot box. Like the evangelical pressure groups of the 1980s, the Klan often swung the balance in electing or defeating county commissioners and members of Congress, state legislatures, city councils, and school boards.

Mayors, sheriffs, and police officers were frequently dues-paying members. Openly or covertly, ambitious politicians courted the Klan's favor. It at one time included a future justice of the U.S. Supreme Court, Hugo L. Black. Among its prospective members was a future president of the United States, Harry S. Truman, who soon turned against it. (Justice Black had joined the Klan while still a young politician in Alabama but later renounced it. Truman in 1922 was running for a county judgeship in Independence, Missouri, when his allies advised him to seek Klan support. Some reports say he handed over his ten-dollar initiation fee, but when asked to promise not to appoint any Roman Catholics in his jurisdiction he angrily withdrew and got his money back. Truman denied he was ever a Klan member.)

The Klan's upper-class roster was not limited to politicians. Gutzon Borglum, the famed sculptor who designed the stone faces of four U.S. presidents on South Dakota's Mount Rushmore, was once a member of the Klan's Imperial Kloncilium—its cabinet—and a confidante of Grand Dragon Stephenson. Lothrop Stoddard, a widely read author (*Scientific Humanism, The Rising Tide of Color*) was a Klan officer in Massachusetts and a ready source for many of the Klan's racial beliefs.[12] Walter Bossert, who obtained

6

his law degree from Indiana University, became a second Klan grand dragon. Circuit court judge Clarence Dearth of Muncie, Indiana, was impeached by the state legislature after his pro-Klan moral zealotry led him into gross judicial misconduct.

The spark that set off a new blast of what Randel called "the Klan spirit" in the early 1920s was a sudden wave of social and moral change in American life following World War I—jazz music, short skirts, teenage boozing, open adultery. (It would later be satirized in the Cole Porter show-title song "Anything Goes.")

Just behind it lay fears of new hordes of unassimilated "aliens." In the years from 1901 to 1920 some 14 million new immigrants had arrived in the United States, including more than 5 million Italian Catholics and Russian Jews. Jazz Age sin and masses of foreigners were both seen as threats to old-line American Protestant values, and the Klan arose in a flag-waving defense of those values.

A 1927 *New Republic* article reviewing the phenomenal spread of the Ku Klux Klan saw it largely as a protest movement:

> To many Americans of the class which contained the largest number of potential members of the Klan, the whole present-day civilization seemed undesirable, as compared with the final days of the Victorian era in which they grew up. Probably they did not consciously expect to turn the clock back, but their mood was one of protest and they were glad of an opportunity to register that fact. The Klan was not an organization seeking to get things done; it was intent on preserving a *status-quo* which seemed in danger of disappearing.[13]

The Klan's targets in the Roaring Twenties included bootleggers, sexual promiscuity, and "immoral" books and movies. One Klan weekly newspaper editor sounded a dominant appeal when he wrote, "[The Klan] is going to drive the bootleggers forever out of this land." And in words familiar to today's Religious Right he added, "It is going to

bring clean moving pictures to this country; It is going to
bring clean literature to this country; It is going to break
up roadside parking, and see that the young man who
induces a girl to get drunk is held accountable."[14]

Anti-black racism was not the dominant, one-track appeal of the 1920s Klan that it had been and would be for
other Klan movements. But it played a substantial role.
World War I had opened new horizons for many blacks, and
there was a growing feeling among whites that new tactics
would be needed to "keep them in their place."

As Arnold Rice wrote:

> The bearing of arms and the freedom of contact with
> whites in France by Negro servicemen and the receiving of
> high wages by many Negroes of the South who moved up to
> northern cities in order to work for war industries made the
> colored people of the nation feel a human dignity they had
> never before experienced. During the 1920s this served to
> increase hostility on the part of whites and to decrease the
> endurance of such hostility on the part of Negroes. The Klan
> was quick to capitalize on the feeling of those whites who
> believed they saw everywhere Negro "uppitiness."[15]

It was out of this mélange of racism, flag-waving patriotism, fundamentalist religion, temperance, anti-Semitism,
and, above all, anti-Catholicism—that D. C. Stephenson
rose to power. As Grand Dragon of the Klan's Indiana realm
and with Klan "propagation rights" in twenty other northern states, he was, before his fall, the Klan's most powerful
figure north of the Mason-Dixon line.

From an eight-room suite of his coal company offices in
downtown Indianapolis, through a highly organized Klan
political machine that reached into every precinct in the
state, he could and often did dictate victory or defeat for his
allies or enemies. Along with Ed Jackson, the new closet
Klansman governor, hundreds of Klan members and allies
in the state legislature owed their jobs to Stephenson. A
Republican Klan puppet was now mayor of Indianapolis.
With a loyal Klan following that included county commis-

sioners, members of city and town councils, sheriffs and police officers, along with hundreds of police auxiliaries legally deputized and armed in a revived "Horse Thief Detective's Association," Stephenson had considerable justification when he said, "I am the law in Indiana."

His plan for the Klan to buy and take over Indiana's Valparaiso University was frustrated by the Klan's national headquarters and the university itself. But by late 1924 he had his eye on a possible U.S. Senate seat (through an appointment by his governor-ally to fill an expected vacancy). And from that base he hoped to capture the 1928 Republican nomination for president of the United States.

From his share in Klan membership fees, his profits on the sale of Klan regalia in Indiana and other northern realms, and his political pay-offs, he became a multimillionaire by the age of thirty-three. He lived high, with a palatial mansion in suburban Indianapolis, a fleet of Cadillacs, and personal bodyguards. He traveled in his own private airplane with personal pilot, and vacationed aboard his luxurious yacht on Lake Erie.

The gospel then being spread by Klan apostles was for him surely only a means to an end: wealth and power, especially the latter. One can hardly believe he really thought the pope was on his way to take over America; that he revered or even read the Bible; that he was shocked by sexual promiscuity or bootleg booze. In fact—long unknown to his host of admirers—this leader of a crusade against sin and the Demon Rum was a covert alcoholic and a compulsive lecher. His mansion was often the scene of wild night orgies.

Still, he could project an image of piety and dedication. Court Asher, a one-time Indiana bootlegger and Stephenson sidekick, recalled some of their visits to church together: "Sometimes we'd leave a wild party, slip into the robes and go into a church to pray with a bunch of Klansmen. Sometimes if the take was real good, we might give them back as much as fifty dollars of their own money. . . . Stephenson could kneel down and pray as convincingly as any minister, [but] when he was in his cups no woman was safe from him."[16] In the end it was his uncontrolled lusts that led to a life sentence for murder and, more than anything else, precipitated the downfall of the Ku Klux Klan in the Middle West.

By spring 1925, the Middle Western Klan had reached its peak of strength. From the hills of southern Indiana to the shores of the Great Lakes, from the farmlands of Kansas to the factory towns of eastern Ohio, flaming crosses and parades of robed and hooded men had become familiar sights.

Stephenson's Indiana was its major arena. Here—with an estimated membership of well over a quarter-million of the state's three million people, with a closet Klansman governor and control of the legislature, with Klan members entrenched in dozens of county, town, and city offices—the Invisible Empire had taken its strongest hold in the North. How and why all of this happened in Indiana—the American heartland of James Whitcomb Riley and "Little Orphant [sic] Annie," a state that in the same decade nurtured Cole Porter, Booth Tarkington, George Ade, and Hoagy Carmichael's "Stardust"—may have many explanations. Certainly the hoods and robes and mysterious rituals offered a change from the monotony of small town life in the 1920s, as did the parades and barbecues and all-day outings where the Klan attracted so many new members. More than half of Indiana's population then lived in communities of 2,500 or less, and usually a Klan parade or picnic was the only show in town.

But these alone could never have enlisted nearly a tenth of the state's population, including thousands in cities like Indianapolis, Evansville, and Fort Wayne. Beneath it all lay a siege mentality, a fear of being engulfed by something other than "our kind" of people. From national Klan headquarters in Atlanta, the new Klan's first Imperial Wizard, "Colonel" William Simmons, had early sounded the alarm, warning, among other things, of "the tremendous influx of foreign immigration, tutored in alien dogmas and alien creeds . . . slowly pushing the native-born, white American into the center of the country, there to be ultimately overwhelmed and smothered."[17]

Catholics, even second- and third-generation American, were, in Indiana as elsewhere, the Klan's major "foreign" threats, tutored as they were in "alien creeds" from Rome. They were still a minority. But as David Chalmers wrote, "To a highly-fragmented, disorganized Protestant America, the Catholic [church] constituted a tightly-organized, well-financed fighting force. The diverse legions of Protestantism saw themselves under attack and that meant America in danger. . . Where the Klan could seize upon this sense of being an embattled minority, its membership rolls soared."[18]

Ironically, most of the "un-American" threats the Klan of Middle America rose to meet—Catholics, Jews, foreigners—were still far away from Klan country, concentrated in large metropolitan areas like New York or Boston. Even Chicagoans had little or no contact with rural or provincial Indiana where the Klan flourished. However, as Norman F. Weaver has pointed out, close cultural confrontation is not necessary to arouse antagonisms. The cultural unity of Indiana itself provided a fertile field. "The homogeneity of Indiana," he said, "is its most striking feature. The Klan had only to seek out the values of that [culturally unified] group and success was practically certain."[19]

Some Indiana communities openly prided themselves on WASP purity. One booster sheet for the town of Mentone, in Kosciusko County (named for a Polish Catholic who helped America win its independence), listed among its advantages that "with a population of 1,700, Mentone has not a Catholic, foreigner, Negro nor Jew in the city."[20] If Mentone boasted of having none of these people, it obviously didn't want any. And if other communities had only a few, they didn't want any more. Some small towns had signs saying, "Nigger, don't let the sun set on you here tonight."

Along with racial and religious bigotry, strong residues of the Puritanism that had come west not far behind the frontier provided an impetus for the Klan. Guilt-ridden by their secret fleshly desires, provincial small town residents often found relief in condemning and harassing "sinners."

A major catalyst for it all was surely the flag-waving hysteria left over from World War I, recently ended. During the war patriotism had been worked up to a fever pitch, sometimes with outrageous propaganda. Now the war was over but the flag-waving spirit continued, looking for some new focus.

Along with this, the Klan made masses of what Imperial Wizard Evans called "the plain people" feel important as saviors of the nation. In portraying the Klan as the champion of Americanism, he wrote in the *North American Review*:

> We are a movement of the plain people, very weak in the matter of culture, intellectual support and trained leadership. We are demanding, and we expect to win, a return of power into the hands of the everyday, not highly cultured, not overly intellectualized, but entirely unspoiled and not de-Americanized, average citizen of the old stock. Our members and leaders are all of this class—the opposite of the intellectuals and liberals who held the leadership and who betrayed Americanism.[21]

Whatever it was, Indiana was not unique. It was simply a more ample, more receptive field for what was going on in many other states. As such it presents perhaps the most illuminating case study of a misguided moral and patriotic crusade that got out of hand, left so much bitterness, and injured so many people—politically, economically, and socially—before it finally ran its course.

The course, in fact, had been abruptly turned by the Stephenson scandal. The public unveiling of the idol of a new moral crusade as a drunken, sadistic rapist destroyed the Klan in Middle America. Politicians who had once

courted its favor now ran for cover. But as he left the jail at
4:00 A.M. on November 21, 1925, Stephenson exuded an
aura of cheer and hope seldom seen in convicted felons
leaving for a prison term. He was not handcuffed. Jail
inmates and officials had arisen early to see his departure.
In its issue of that day, the *Noblesville Daily Ledger* reported:

> With the same buoyant spirit and smile which made him so
> popular in Indiana during the height of his public career
> and with a handshake with every prisoner in jail and also
> every member of the sheriff's family, D. C. Stephenson,
> convicted of the murder of Miss Madge Oberholtzer, left
> Noblesville for the Indiana State Prison at Michigan City to
> begin the life sentence imposed on him by a local jury a
> week ago.

A barber had been called to the jail the day before to give
Stephenson a shave and haircut. The *Ledger* reported that,
dressed in a brown business suit, "he presented a neat
appearance when he stepped into the ante room of the jail
and started out the west entrance of the building to get into
the automobile."

He had asked for thirty days of free time to arrange his
business affairs before starting his prison term but was
denied. On the evening of the day before he left the jail, he
had met with reporters and issued a statement ridiculing
this refusal and insisted he had been the victim of "persecution." He said:

> What have I to run from? And from whom in that small
> group of selfish and zero-intellect individuals who have
> arrayed themselves against me—some through envy—some
> through jealousy—some through fear—some through politi-
> cal disappointment?
>
> If there ever has been any doubt in the public mind (and
> I refer here only to the intelligent people), as to whether
> this has been persecution or prosecution, I believe every
> atom of that doubt will be swept away by the lustful haste
> with which so-called orderly procedure of courts has sent

13

me to Michigan City . . . for no reason but to deny me the right of advice by counsel and to stifle my resources in arranging my business affairs to meet this unjust contingency.

And for what? To satisfy the clamor of the common herd, whose opinion is the exception to prove the rule that the preponderance of public opinion will forever condemn the injustice, unfairness, and downright dishonesty of this malicious propaganda campaign from its beginning, which would be laughable were it not for the tragic ending. Every fair-minded citizen will accept this as common sense.[22]

As he approached the prison gates, the former Grand Dragon clung to delusions of his former power. He was confident he would not be behind bars for long. The murder verdict had been at least questionable. His rape victim had, in fact, taken poison by her own hand after the attack. Many still believed her death was suicide rather than murder. Also, some felt, the public uproar surrounding the case had hardly been conducive to calm, objective jurisprudence. Threats against his life—so Stephenson claimed— had kept him from taking the witness stand in his own defense.

There was room, he believed, for a pardon or commutation, and he felt it would soon come from his longtime ally, the man who owed him so much—Governor Ed Jackson.

He was wrong. But ultimately he would have his revenge.

1

Evansville: Bridgehead on the Ohio

THE NEW KU KLUX KLAN that was soon to spread through the American Middle West built its first bridgehead in Indiana in 1921. It began in Evansville, just across the Ohio River from Kentucky. Here, only about a year earlier, D. C. Stephenson—a one-time wandering printer, aged twenty nine, recently out of the World War I army— had arrived as a newcomer to the state.

The future Grand Dragon had not come to organize the Klan. He had only been looking for a business opportunity and soon found it as a partner in a small but prosperous coal business. There is, in fact, no evidence that he had, on his arrival in Evansville, any special interest in the Klan or its goals. And Evansville itself, at first glance, would have hardly seemed to be promising Klan country.

Had the hooded Knights of the Invisible Empire been looking for some place to rescue a white, Anglo-Saxon, Protestant society from being overrun by "alien forces," they could hardly have chosen a more unlikely locale. Out of Evansville's total population of about 85,000, some 76,000 were native-born white Americans. Almost 65,000 of these were of old-stock native parentage. Foreign-born white "aliens" numbered only about 3,000. In eighty-five of

Indiana's ninety-two counties in 1920, foreign-born residents made up less than 5 percent of the population. (Lake County, abutting Chicago in the far north, was a major exception, with an estimated 25 to 35 percent foreign-born). Blacks in Evansville totaled fewer than 6,000, few if any of them openly militant.

Roman Catholics, who became the Klan's chief target, were barely visible. The entire Catholic population of Indiana was then only about 300,000 in a state of some three million people—most of them in areas far to the north. In the hills of southern Indiana there was probably not more than one Catholic family in 100.

Clearly, the same provincial WASP culture that pervaded most of Indiana was firmly established here. Yet, on the surface, Evansville was hardly provincial Indiana. Its face was one of progress and change, a bustling, growing industrial city with new factories spreading rapidly around the north bank of the big bend in the Ohio River. Where men had once cut lumber or made furniture or cast-iron stoves, they were now earning better wages manufacturing truck bodies, automobiles, auto parts, and newfangled "electric ice boxes."

The Graham Brothers Truck Company, with a half-million square feet of floor space, was the city's biggest industry, turning out truck bodies by the hundreds and fitting them with Dodge engines from Detroit. Graham would soon become the nation's second-largest truck producer and to trucks would be added a new line of passenger cars—the Graham-Paige. Experiments with cooling coils had brought the new electric refrigerator to a society where almost everyone had bought ice from horse-drawn delivery wagons. Soon an Evansville manufacturer called Serv-El ("Serve Electrically") would become a major employer and pioneer a new line of gas refrigerators.

Economically the spirit was one of progress and change, but this was not reflected in the dominant culture. Unlike the state's big steel and smokestack complexes in cities in the far north—Gary, Hammond, and East Chicago—where the foreign-born might number as high as 30 percent, Evansville's labor force was fed by the native population, largely conservative, old-stock Protestant folk with roots in the southern hills. Indiana had, in fact, been populated "from the bottom up," with the bulk of its early settlers coming west and north from Virginia and Kentucky.

However, generations of roistering Ohio river boatmen had left a strong residue of sin: gambling, whiskey-swilling, brothels. By 1898 one Evansville whorehouse madam had become the inspiration for Paul Dresser's Broadway hit song "My Gal Sal." (Annie Brace [sic], known to her customers as "Sallie Walker," was once Paul Dresser's mistress in Evansville. The relationship is described by Dresser's brother, Theodore Dreiser, in his autobiography, *Dawn*. Dreiser was the family name; Paul took "Dresser" as a show business name.)

Indiana had its own Prohibition law banning alcoholic drinks in 1919, a year before the Eighteenth Amendment went into effect, but Kentucky remained "wet" to the last. From a pier at the foot of Evansville's Main Street, peak-traffic ferries left every half-hour carrying drinkers to a boozy resort called White City on the other shore.

As the Klan arrived, bootleggers, brothel keepers, and gamblers shared the same turf with religious fundamentalists and rigid moralists; with a Methodist church that could still expel members for dancing or card playing, and where Sunday dances were forbidden by law. In spring 1920, the *Evansville Courier* reported fourteen arrests by U.S. marshals cracking down on an Evansville whiskey ring and predicted the total would be more than eighty.[1] A few days earlier, the same newspaper also reported that the district's Methodist ministers had just passed a resolution opposing any changes in the church's "amusement ban." Some changes might be in order, the ministers acknowledged, but they might open the way to approval of dances—which the newspaper said was "the recreation most obnoxious to the ministers."[2]

While fundamentalist pastors inveighed against carnality and fornication in the back seats of automobiles, drinking, petting parties, and lovers' lanes were increasing. Teenagers who would never have been allowed inside a pre-Prohibition saloon were now buying bottles of moonshine liquor in back alleys or hillside shacks. Skirts were getting shorter and the beat of jazz (once a four-letter word) was getting louder.

Along with all of this came the strong current of nativist patriotism, left over from the war so recently ended. It was both flag-waving and isolationist. We had turned the tide in France and proved our virtue and valor, but never again. Let Europe fight its own wars from now on. Even the American tourist of a popular poem found no permanent attractions there. It was "home again, and home again, America for me!"

War veterans were glad to be home from the War to End War—later more often called the "war to end all wars." The accepted belief was that most of them didn't want to talk about it. Still, they had an aura of distinction they would never have had without it. They had their organizations and romantic reunions and were becoming a political force.

Into this milieu of materialistic progress, old-time religion, sin, and nativist patriotism came, sometime in 1920, Joseph M. Huffington, a Ku Klux Klan organizer from Tulsa. He arrived with the support and direction of national Klan headquarters in Atlanta and Imperial Wizard "Colonel" William J. Simmons.

The new Ku Klux Klan, a revival of the original white supremacist group in the Reconstruction South, was then about five years old. On Thanksgiving eve, 1915, Simmons had gathered a small group of followers on Stone Mountain, near Atlanta, and, as he said later, "under a blazing cross (a wooden cross padded with excelsior and soaked in kerosene) the Invisible Empire was called from its slumber of half a century to take up a new task and fulfill a new mission for humanity's good and to call back to mortal habitation the good angel of practical fraternity among men."[3]

The first Ku Klux Klan, which had slumbered so long, originated in December 1865, less than a year after the Civil War, in the little town of Pulaski, Tennessee—with little or no indication of what it was to become. It began, in fact, as a small social club organized by six young former Confederate officers, bored with small-town life and looking for something to do.

The words *Ku Klux* they adapted from *kuklos*, a variant of the Greek *kyklos* meaning cycle or circle—in their case their own little circle. For alliteration a young former captain named John B. Kennedy suggested adding *Klan*, possibly from romantic visions of the old Scottish clans portrayed by Sir Walter Scott, then one of the South's most popular authors. For picaresque fun they adopted mystical language and initiation rites, along with costumes of hoods and flowing robes. Any night could be Halloween as they rode through the little town to stir up some excitement.

Meanwhile, however, in communities through the defeated South, other groups were forming with a more serious purpose. Faced with hordes of newly freed black slaves and an invasion of northern carpetbag politicians, vigilante groups and armed patrols were organizing in self-defense. They went by various names: Men of Justice, Pale Faces, White Brotherhood, Order of White Rose, Knights of the White Camelia.

Soon the Klan, with its mysterious regalia and symbols, was seen as a vehicle for maintaining white supremacy. Masked night riders in flowing robes, with skulls dangling from saddles, pretending to be the ghosts of dead Confederate soldiers, could terrify superstitious "darkies" and "keep them in their place."

The Klan soon became the leader among the white supremacist groups, and many were united in its ranks. Its program was formulated and extended at a meeting in Nashville in April 1867. General Nathan Bedford Forrest, a widely respected former Confederate officer, was elected as its leader, with the title of "Grand Wizard." Forrest took an active part in organizing Klan units, especially in opposition to the Reconstruction acts of a vengeful radical Republican Congress.

The Klan soon spread throughout the South. In many sketches of early Klansmen, white crosses appeared on their hoods. But the flaming cross symbol, which had so much significance for the fundamentalist Klan of the 1920s, apparently did not originate with the first Klan. Available drawings and recruiting posters of the time show no such displays.

Some writers have speculated that the flaming cross idea came from similar crosses once used to rally clans in the old Scottish Highlands. (The American Order of Scottish Clans had a publication called the *Fiery Cross* and once brought an unsuccessful action against the Indiana Klan for using the same name on its periodical.) However, all records indicate that Colonel Simmons was the first to use a flaming cross, beginning with the Stone Mountain Ceremony in 1915, and its use is probably due more to his background as a onetime Methodist revivalist than to any Scottish influence.

Masked night riders and "ghosts" did affect some blacks, but not all. Soon some Klansmen adopted more violent tactics, such as whippings and murders. At the same time common criminals began to use Klan regalia as a cloak for their own crimes of robbery, rape, or arson. The excesses turned many upper-class southerners against the Klan. Finally, in 1869, General Forrest ordered that "masks and costumes of this order [the Klan] be entirely abolished and destroyed." Remnants remained, but by 1872, after two congressional investigations and amidst a growing confidence among southern whites that they were not going to be obliterated, the Klan was fast disappearing.

When in 1915 Simmons called its "angel" back to "mortal habitation," he was thirty-five years old and a professional

The Ku Klux Klan began in 1865 as a small social club in Pulaski, Tennessee. To the left is the widow of one of the founders, ex-Confederate Captain John B. Kennedy. The Klan quickly outgrew its original quarters, and its purpose changed. (Klanwatch S.P.L.C.)

Klansmen about to
lynch John Camp-
bell, a "confessed Re-
publican," 1871. He
was rescued by fed-
eral agents. (Culver
Pictures)

Confederate General
Nathan Bedford Forrest
became first head of the
expanded Klan in 1867,
with the title of Grand
Wizard. (Library of
Congress)

The southern vision of the Klan as champion of white supremacy over newly-freed slaves is shown in this popular poster from the late 1860s. (Rutherford B. Hayes Presidential Center)

"Colonel" William J. Simmons, who revived the Ku Klux Klan in 1915. (Culver Pictures)

lodge organizer. Born on a farm near Harpersville, Alabama, he had grown up steeped in Civil War romanticism and stories of the old Klan. He had served in the First Alabama Volunteers in the Spanish-American War (but not as a colonel). He had once tried to become a Methodist minister, but after a tour on revival circuits he had been denied a pulpit by the Alabama Conference of Churches.

He turned briefly to commercial sales, then to the founding and organization of fraternal groups. His title of colonel came from his command of regiments in the Woodmen of the World. When asked his profession, he usually replied, "fraternalist."

It was perhaps inevitable that he would dream of founding a new lodge of his own, and his thoughts soon turned to a revival of the Ku Klux Klan. He was surely influenced by *The Birth of a Nation*, D. W. Griffith's classic silent movie based on Thomas Dixon, Jr.'s romantic novel *The Clansman*.

Dixon, a one-time student at Johns Hopkins University and a friend and classmate of future president Woodrow Wilson, had grown up in North Carolina in the Reconstruction South. He had been a North Carolina legislator and a Baptist minister, but finally found his most rewarding outlet in writing fiction.

In 1905 he published *The Clansman*, subtitled *An Historical Romance of the Ku Klux Klan*. It begins as a contrived love story: Ben Cameron, a young Confederate colonel, is being nursed in a Union prison hospital by Elsie Stoneman, sister of the Union officer who captured him. They fall in love. Then Elsie's brother, Phil Stoneman, falls in love with Ben's sister. Such love bodes well for a reunion of North and South, but this happy prospect is soon shattered by Phil and Elsie's father, Congressman Stoneman (a copy of Thaddeus Stevens) who is determined to have revenge on the South. His instrument is to be black people, manipulated to dominate white civilization.

Blacks take over southern legislatures and property. They lust after white women. President Lincoln, who had urged "malice toward none," is dead. The south has lost its last protector. The Klan arises in self-defense. Ben Cameron becomes a Grand Dragon in the Carolinas. The Black Tide is stemmed. Southern civilization is saved.

Soon Dixon adapted the book to the stage and took a leading role in several touring company versions. He thought of making a movie but never got it going. Finally, he attracted the attention of Griffith, then a young director with the Biograph Company. Griffith took the basic Dixon scenario, added historical background, and produced a classic.

The movie had its première in New York City on March 3, 1915. By the time it arrived in Atlanta on December 1, it was already a controversial hit. The film lasted two hours and forty-five minutes. It first showed a serene, happy antebellum South, the arrival of black bond servants, their placid life on plantations. Then came the abolitionists, then the secessionists, then the war.

A thirty-piece pit orchestra interspersed black spirituals with Wagner throughout battle scenes depicting returning soldiers, barefoot illiterate blacks sitting in state legislatures, and a white girl (played by Lillian Gish) besieged in her cabin by lust-crazed black men. As the orchestra played passages from *Die Walküre*, the hooded, robed Klansmen assembled. Then, as the music shifted to Grieg's *Hall of the Mountain King*, they rode to the rescue.

To many, including Griffith himself, the film was an honest portrayal of conditions in the postwar South. But to many others it was inflammatory propaganda. In New York audiences threw eggs at the screen. In Boston the movie provoked a near-riot. In Atlanta, however, it was assured a warm reception, with sellout crowds at the then-steep price of two dollars per ticket.

Simmons saw the film as a launching pad for his new Ku Klux Klan. A week before the film's Atlanta opening, he had assembled some forty followers from his various lodges for an organizational meeting in the city's Piedmont Hotel. Those who expected only a hotel session were soon surprised to find Simmons had hired a sight-seeing bus to take them to Stone Mountain, about sixteen miles away.

It was a cold Thanksgiving eve, and not all were eager for the trip. Only a few went along. Carrying flashlights they made their way up the mountain slab, where the cross was lit and the Klan "reborn." In the same Atlanta Journal of December 7, 1915, advertising *The Birth of a Nation*, Simmons had placed an adjacent advertisement announcing his formation of "The World's Greatest Secret, Social, Patriotic, Fraternal, Beneficial Order."

Soon he had nearly 100 followers. The Klan was incorporated as a "benevolent and eleemosynary" institution, with an outward appearance not too much different from the Elks or Odd Fellows. Its earliest members were solid middle-class citizens, including a future congressman, Robert Ramspect, and a Fulton County commissioner, Paul Etheridge. At first there was no night riding. The first image of the new Klan was that of just another lodge that stressed patriotism and the exclusiveness of the white race. It was Protestant, but not openly anti-Catholic or anti-Semitic. Many lodges then and for decades later had racial and religious restrictions on membership.

With U.S. entry into World War I in 1917, Simmons's Klan found an outlet for more aggressive action. Alien enemies, "slackers," and strike leaders became targets. Robed Klansmen openly tried to put down a shipyard strike in Mobile. Sometimes they marched in full regalia in flag-waving parades.

Meanwhile, Simmons began looking for new apostles to spread the Klan gospel. He found two of the most effective ones in a former newspaperman, Edward Y. Clarke, and Elizabeth Tyler, who together operated the Southern Publicity Association. They had successfully raised money for such varied causes as the Anti-Saloon League, the Roosevelt Memorial, and Near East Relief.

Soon Clarke and Bessie Tyler launched a nationwide propaganda and organizing campaign. The country was divided into Klan domains—or geographical areas—such as the Southeast, Southwest, Northeast, Mississippi Valley, and Pacific Coast. Organizers and recruiters were called "Kleagles." As national head of the promotional effort, Clarke became Imperial Kleagle, or top promoter. Organizing directors of state realms were called King Kleagles, under a Grand Goblin who ruled the domain. Rank-and-file, house-to-house solicitors were simply Kleagles. (By this time Colonel Simmons, as top man of the Klan, had become Imperial Wizard.)

Money played a large part in inspiring the workers. The Klan membership fee was ten dollars. Usually four of those dollars went to the Kleagle, the local solicitor, when he signed up a new member. One dollar went to the King Kleagle, the state sales manager. The Grand Goblin got only fifty cents, and the remaining $4.50 went to national Klan headquarters in Atlanta. This original apportionment underwent later variations, but it shows the general pattern of financial incentive.

Yet the incentive was not entirely financial. The commercial motive, Mecklin observed, "plays a part naturally and inevitably in every such system of promotion. But it must not be forgotten that the commercial motive alone can never explain the . . . spread of the Klan."[4]

As the Klan grew and internal rivalries appeared, Simmons was becoming more militant and outspoken. Preparing to address one meeting of Georgia Klansmen, Simmons

> silently took a Colt automatic from his pocket and placed it on the table in front of him. Then he took a revolver from another pocket and put it on the table too. Then he unbuckled his cartridge belt and draped it in a crescent shape between the two weapons. Next, still without uttering a word, he drew out a bowie knife and plunged it into the center of things on the table [then said] 'Now let the niggers, the Catholics, Jews and all who disdain my imperial wizardry come on.' "[5]

By this time Simmons was known to be drinking heavily, and alcohol quite probably influenced his behavior.

He often denounced "mongrel civilizations" and said the Japanese, then a growing target of restrictive immigration policies, were only a "superior colored race." At the same time he opened the way for a new wave of anti-Catholicism, and this, more than anything else, fueled the growth of the Klan. Hordes of new Catholic immigrants from Europe, the Klan feared, were threatening to take over America for the Pope of Rome. Soon the Klan's un-American targets grew to include local and personal immorality—bootleg booze, dope, sexual promiscuity, night clubs, roadhouses.

By summer 1921, the national membership of the Klan had grown to about 100,000. It was still mostly in the South and Southwest, but Huffington had already established the Klan's first Indiana Klavern—a local Klan meeting place— in Evansville. By September of the same year, the *New York World* had begun its series of exposés of Klan violence. Between October 1920 and October 1921, the *World* documented more than 100 atrocities and aggressions associated with the Klan in the South and Southwest: four killings, one mutilation, one acid-branding (KKK inscribed on the forehead), forty-one floggings, twenty-seven tar-and-feather parties, five kidnappings, and forty-three individuals warned to leave town or otherwise threatened.

The series brought pressure for a congressional investigation, undertaken by the House Rules Committee in October 1921. Summoned to Washington, D.C., Imperial Wizard Simmons strongly disclaimed Klan involvement in the reported violence. He steadfastly maintained that the Klan was a purely fraternal and patriotic organization. He said he thought the violence was the work of people trying to discredit the Klan, but that if they were Klansmen they were violating Klan principles of law and order. Nothing of substance came out of the inquiry, and the Klan continued to grow.

Many students of the Klan phenomenon feel that *World* exposés, well intentioned and well documented as they were, actually helped rather than hindered the Klan. Chalmers says "the series increased the *World*'s sales by a hundred thousand. It increased Klan sales by ten times that number."[6]

The *World* and other newspapers, he believes, had seen only the commercial motives of the Klan founders and the violence of some members. Like Mecklin, he says they misunderstood the basic emotional appeal of the Klan to the Middle-American mind of the 1920s—an appeal that made many distrust attacks by the press.

A 1923 *Baltimore Sun* exposé of atrocities and miscarriages of justice in Morehouse Parish, Louisiana, seems, likewise, to have had no restraint on Klan growth. Despite evidence of the torture and brutal murders of two white men in a Klan ambush, a grand jury had refused to indict the accused. The *Sun* showed much Klan influence in the whole affair, but in the same year Klan membership increased by the thousands.

E. H. Loucks, in his study of the Klan in Pennsylvania, says one reason prospective Klansmen disregarded the newspaper attacks was that they came from big city papers. Whatever New York attacked, he said, rural and small-town America, with its defensive inferiority complex, would support.[7]

The Ku Klux Klan's "first public appearance" in Evansville, as it was called in the local press, came at the Central Methodist Episcopal Church, at 300 Mary Street, on the Sunday night of March 26, 1922. The church was crowded. The first hymn had been sung and the pastor, the Reverend A. M. Couchman, was about to deliver his sermon.

Suddenly the doors opened and about twenty masked men robed in white from head to foot entered and marched up the aisle single file. They knelt at the altar for a few seconds in silent prayer. Then their spokesman turned to the Reverend Couchman and said, "In the interest of the work you are doing in the church we present you with this sum of money." It amounted to twenty-five dollars in bills.

They left the church without a further word, climbed into automobiles with covered license plates, and drove away. The Reverend Couchman resumed the service without reference to the Klan visit, but after the services were over men and women remained in groups discussing the visit of the mysterious strangers.[8]

As the weeks went on the recruiting continued. By early June 1922, the Evansville Klan was ready to make its big splash. A quarter-page ad in the *Courier* read:

What is the
Ku Klux Klan?
Dr. Caleb Ridley, Ph.D.
of Atlanta, Ga.
Will Tell You at an
OPEN MEETING
FRIDAY NIGHT JUNE 9 AT 8 P.M.
at the
COLISEUM

Everybody Invited   Special Invitation Extended to Ladies

On this Friday night in June at least 6,000 people, including some 2,000 standees, gathered in the Evansville Coliseum. Without doubt many had come out of sheer curiosity, but they were soon caught up in the mixture of flag waving and old-time religion that was to characterize so many Klan rallies across the state.

The meeting had been preceded by a parade of hooded Klansmen down Main Street to Fourth and over to the Coliseum, led by a fiery cross, a huge American flag, and a rider on horseback. About fifty of the robed, masked Klansmen were seated on the Coliseum platform. One knelt and kissed the flag. Others moved through the audience passing out programs enunciating the Klan creed and the words of a song, " 'Tis the Old Time Religion," to be sung at the end of the meeting.

While the audience waited to hear Dr. Ridley it was entertained by a quartet known as the Hutchison Brothers. The quartet sang a popular ditty, "If you don't like your Uncle Sammy . . ." guaranteed to touch the heartstrings of provincial antialienism with its chorus:

27

If you don't like your Uncle Sammy,
Then go back to your home o'er the sea
To the land from where you came
Whatever be its name,
But don't be ungrateful to me.
If you don't like the stars in Old Glory,
If you don't like the red, white, and blue,
Then don't act like the cur in the story.
Don't bite the hand that's feeding you.

Wild applause followed, bringing back the singers for a third time. Joe Huffington then introduced Dr. Ridley, a national Klan chaplain who had been sent up by Simmons's Klan headquarters in Atlanta.

In a long oration, Dr. Ridley proceeded to define the Klan and its values and goals: "The first principle of the Klan is that it is a white man's organization. Some people think we ought to apologize for it. But we are not going to do it. Some think we are against all who are not white. That is not so. If they attend to their business we'll attend to ours. We are not out gunning for anyone, regardless of his race or creed."[9]

Then came the exclusion of Jews: "It is [a] gentile organization. You know I'm not responsible for being gentile. God almighty takes care of that. Our organization is for white, gentile Americans."

Next the Catholics: The Klan was "first, last and all the time a Protestant organization. That doesn't mean we are bothering anybody about their religion. What we care is that we are not going to mix up with them in this organization."

More on race: "The Klan believes in the supremacy of the Anglo-Saxon race, now and forever. This is a white man's country. The white man discovered this country and laid the foundation for our civilization. . . . God fixed color and when it is crossed some low-down scalawag is interfering with God's business."

On morality and American womanhood: "Klansmen stand for the protection of American womanhood. There is no moral standard in foreign countries now and it is so darn near the same here that it makes us blush sometimes. I think the women are more responsible for the darn moral cussedness of this nation than the men themselves. The Ku Klux Klan has set itself to the high task of protecting the women and making it easy for them to be what the right sort of woman should be."

Language and schools became part of the nativist appeal: "If there is room for only one flag it naturally follows that there is room for only one language." Dr. Ridley said a member of his church in Atlanta who was also a congressman had introduced a bill providing that "every newspaper printed in a foreign language shall run down alongside the columns the same thing translated in English, which I am for." (At this time there were more than 1,000 foreign-language newspapers and periodicals in the United States, including German, Italian, and Yiddish. Most were weeklies, but well over 100 were dailies. Foreign-language publications in the U.S. had reached a peak of 1,300 in 1914, but pressures in World War I forced many German papers to close.)[10]

Just as there was room for only one flag and one language, he continued, "there is only room for one honest-to-God school system in this country. Our public schools are the schools of the nation and no priest or pope has the right, or anyone else has the right to enter in any other system of education." (Catholic schools were to become a major target of proposed restrictive legislation in Indiana and other states. To this end the Klan loudly called for "separation of church and state," but it meant only separation of the Roman Catholic Church from the state. Klansmen saw no conflict when they demanded laws requiring state-mandated prayer and Bible reading in public schools.)

Dr. Ridley urged political—but not "partisan"—action: "The time has come when orations don't do any good. It is through the ballot that we can act. The Klan is not in politics. I mean in partisan politics. But that does not mean that we should not look over the list [of candidates for office] to see who one might or might not vote for." He warned politicians that "red-blooded Americans are here in Evansville" and they could "get your number."

He took pains to dispel the night-riding vigilante image of the Klan portrayed in recent newspaper exposés: "The humblest Klansman in Evansville, if he is a real one, is a better citizen from a law-enforcement standpoint than any man in town, be he priest, preacher or what not who is not a Klansman." He discounted the people portrayed in the *World* series as "riff-raff." Beyond being a white, Anglo-Saxon Protestant, he said, a requisite for Klan membership "contrary to the *New York World* and some local papers, is that you must establish the fact that you are a high-class gentleman or you can't get in."

Extended applause followed Dr. Ridley's address. Then came the finale—a mass chanting of " 'Tis the Old Time Religion" that started feet tapping and hands clapping in time:

> 'tis the old time religion,
> 'tis the old time religion,
> 'tis the old time religion,
> It's good enough for me . . .
> It was good for our fathers . . .
> It was good for the Prophet David . . .
> It was good for the Hebrew children . . .
> It was good in the fiery furnace . . .
> It will take us all to heaven,
> And it's good enough for me.

On the day of the Klan rally, the *Courier* had another smaller Klan story on an inside page: "30 Klansmen Indicted. California KKK's Surrender." The California Klansmen had been charged with kidnapping, false imprisonment, and assault with intent to commit murder in connection with a vigilante raid on a suspected Hispanic bootlegger at Inglewood, near Los Angeles.[11]

It was all far away. The Ku Klux Klan had arrived in

Indiana wrapped in the flag and a mantle of morality and law and order. Soon its crosses would be burning from Vincennes to Fort Wayne, from New Albany to Valparaiso, and powerful political forces would be at its beck and call.

2

Steve: Birth of a Salesman

BY THE TIME of the Klan's Coliseum rally, David Curtis Stephenson—the future Grand Dragon, who would boast, "I am the law in Indiana"—had been in Evansville a little more than two years.

He had arrived in early 1920, only about a year after his discharge from the army in Massachusetts. His last stop had been Akron, Ohio, where he had sold linotype machines and made a brief, unsuccessful attempt to start a newspaper.

Akron was only a way station in what had been a wandering life. Born in Houston, on August 21, 1891, he had come as a child with his family to Maysville, Oklahoma. He had entered the printer's trade as a teenager, worked as a typesetter in more than ten small Oklahoma towns, dabbled in Socialist politics, then moved to Iowa. It was here, in Boone, Iowa, that he joined the National Guard in early 1917, moving into federal service when America entered the war a few months later.

At first there seemed to be no direct connection between the Evansville Klan and the man who was to become one of the Invisible Empire's most powerful figures. He apparently began as a salesman. The 1920 Evansville city directory lists one "David C. Stephenson" as "salsmn mngr, Ames Mnfg. Co." living at the "Vendome Hotel." He was soon, however, into coal stocks, then in the coal business with a partner, L. G. Julian. But before long his salesman's mind also turned to politics, with fellow army veterans as an organizing base.

He was not a decorated war hero. A story widely circulated among Klansmen was that he had fought in France as a major. Actually, all of his military service had been in the United States, and his highest rank was second lieutenant in Company D of the 36th Infantry, when he was honorably discharged in February 1919 at Camp Devens, Massachusetts.

In appearance he was hardly striking; he was rather chubby-faced, stocky (5 feet, 10 inches tall, and about 170 pounds). Still, as John Bartlow Martin describes him, "he was handsome, with blond hair, thin, plucked eyebrows, a thin mouth, steady blue-grey eyes, and a ready smile. He dressed conservatively and looked, like, say a banker."[1]

A reporter who visited him in his Indianapolis office in 1924 described him as "an affable young man with a smooth-shaven, full face, ruddy complexion and a prosperous double-chin, quietly but carefully dressed. His movements are decisive and energetic, his speech brisk and incisive—a typical, dynamic young executive."[2] Perhaps most importantly, as Norman Weaver said, he had "a powerful voice, and was a natural actor and orator. He was capable of making an audience believe statements that, when read, sounded absurd or foolish."[3]

His formal educational background was scanty. He had left school in the eighth grade, shortly after his family came to Oklahoma. Yet his speech was fluent and polished. Edgar Allen Booth, a Klansman who worked closely with Stephenson for more than two years, wrote that "his use of the English language was marvelous when one considers that his [public school] education had ceased when he was in the grammar [eighth grade] school."[4]

In Akron Stephenson had taken a new wife, Violet Mary

Carroll. It was his second marriage. His first had been in 1915 while he worked as a printer in Hugo, Oklahoma. His bride then was Jeanette Hamilton, a young woman who had won a newspaper contest as "the most beautiful girl in Oklahoma." Within two years he deserted her and an infant daughter, moved to Miami, Oklahoma, then, posing as a single man, to Iowa. Shortly after he entered military service, his first wife divorced him. Within two years he was separated from his second.

In Evansville in mid-1920, Stephenson made his first direct pass at political office. He announced his candidacy for the Democratic nomination for Congress. Despite his growing support among war veterans, the professional politicians showed little interest and he went no further. Probably about this time his ambition and his salesman's instincts turned toward the Ku Klux Klan. There is little or no evidence that he was deeply imbued with Klan ideology: overt racism and fears of Catholics taking over America, Jazz Age sin, and bootleggers (he partook freely of their product). In his later public speeches he most often extolled "pure Americanism" and the Constitution. He warned of "foreign influences," but never openly denounced the Pope.

In 1924 he told a magazine reporter during an interview in Indianapolis: "I did not sell the Klan in Indiana on hatreds. That is not my way. I sold the Klan on Americanism and reform. There were two ways of accomplishing this, by the ballot or by direct action. I am a law-abiding citizen, naturally I abhor direct action. I sold the Klan as a political instrument for reform and progress, wholly constructive."[5] Yet, he was obviously aware of the hatreds and outrageous slanders being spread by Klan propagandists down the line and the base they were providing for Klan growth. And, as one writer said in a 1928 article reviewing his career, "Stephenson made no attempt to regulate the propaganda or censor the speeches used by [Klan] lecturers or evangelists. He turned them loose and let them talk."[6]

By fall 1920, after his failure to get on the Democratic primary ballot, Stephenson adroitly switched political directions. Prohibition, though still in its infancy, was already a major issue. Democrats had the reputation of being wet (for repeal of the 18th Amendment) and Republicans dry. The former wet Democrat, sensing the power of the Klan and the Anti-Saloon League, went over to the dry side, urging his veterans to back Republican candidates.

Soon he was in touch with Klan headquarters in Atlanta and became an officially recognized "Kleagle." In the Klan hierarchy then, a King Kleagle was the top organizer for a state realm, which was as yet unchartered. Once the realm received its charter from national headquarters, the King Kleagle became Grand Dragon, a title Stephenson would have by mid-1923.

Joe Huffington continued as head of the Evansville Klan, but he was rapidly eclipsed by Stephenson in the eyes of national Klan officials. By late 1922, Stephenson was a King Kleagle and had brought the Indiana Klan membership up to some five thousand. Atlanta saw him as the Klan's rising star of the North. When, in late November 1922, Imperial Wizard Simmons held his second biennial Klonvocation (Klan national convention) in Atlanta, Stephenson traveled south in a private railway car.

There, as he had expected, a palace revolution was shaping up. Imperial Wizard Simmons seemed to be losing his grip. His organizational leadership had not matched his earlier zeal. He was drinking heavily. In July 1922, the Klan's Imperial Kligrapp (national secretary) had charged that the Klan publicist, E. Y. Clarke, had virtually taken over by taking advantage of Simmons's continual drunken condition.

Clarke himself had earlier caused a scandal when, in October 1919, he and his publicist partner, Bessie Tyler, were arrested together in Atlanta and charged with disorderly conduct—being intoxicated and not fully clad. The *New York World* later described the scene of the arrest as a "house of ill repute." Information leading to the arrest had come from Clarke's wife, who later divorced him, charging desertion. A new, younger Klan faction had decided by late

35

1922 that it was time for Simmons, and possibly also Clarke, to go.

Meanwhile, another Klan star was rising in Texas: Hiram Wesley Evans, a Dallas dentist and Vanderbilt University graduate (class of 1900). Evans, like Simmons, was an active lodge man and a professional organizer and joiner. He had early been attracted to the Klan, and when an anti-Klan movement arose among usually cooperative Texas Masons, he had taken the lead in suppressing it. By the time of the Atlanta Klonvocation he had been a Klan Exalted Cyclops (elected head of a local Klan chapter) in the Dallas area and Great Titan (district head) of a major Texas Klan Province (group of counties), and now had become a Kligrapp (secretary) in Simmons's Imperial Kloncilium.

The Klonvocation's nomination and election of Klan officers was set to begin on the morning of November 27. On the night of the twenty-sixth a small group of rebels gathered in Atlanta's Piedmont Hotel. Among them were Evans; Fred Savage, a former New York City police detective who now, as chief of staff, headed a fifty-man Klan secret police force; H. C. McCall, another Texas Great Titan from Houston; and J. C. Comer, Grand Dragon from Arkansas. They sent word to Stephenson in his private railway car to come and join them.

Soon a plan developed to kick Simmons upstairs with a five-hundred-dollar monthly salary and give his job to Evans. Stephenson suggested one thousand dollars a month, and the others agreed. They decided to approach Simmons immediately. Stephenson and Savage would make the first visit with Evans staying in the background.

About 3:00 A.M., with the opening of convention nominations only about eight hours away, Stephenson and Savage arrived at Simmons's residence, 1840 Peachtree Street, and awakened the Imperial Wizard, who had recently been out drinking. As Simmons told it later, their first question was: Was he going to let his name come before the convention for nomination and election? Simmons said he was not politicking, that he would leave this up to the convention delegates themselves. If the Klan wanted him he would serve.

Savage became more threatening. Don't let your name come before the convention, he told Simmons. There are men there waiting to attack your reputation, and this would be bad for the Klan. (Some accounts say they showed Simmons "compromising photographs" of himself in a drunken condition). If they attacked, Savage said, he would have armed men posted with orders to shoot to kill anyone who started the attacks. This would be a scandal and a serious blow to the Klan movement. To forestall all this, he again appealed to Simmons to refuse to let his name be brought up. As an emergency back-up plan, they proposed that Evans's name be used. Simmons finally agreed, with Evans in only a temporary post until he could get someone more to his liking.[7]

The final outcome was that the delegates were maneuvered into declaring—in effect, retiring—Simmons as "emperor for life" with a $1,000 monthly income. A brief and diverting show was made with a proposal that Clarke be made Imperial Wizard. But, as planned, he declined, accepting instead a title of "Imperial Giant" with a renewal of his Klan sales contract. Clarke was more interested in money than titles. The mantle was then shifted to Evans, who was acclaimed the new Imperial Wizard. A Texas dentist and an Indiana coal merchant, with the aid of a New York detective, had taken over the Ku Klux Klan from its founder.

Stephenson was richly rewarded for his part in the palace revolution. He returned north as Atlanta's representative for the Klan in Indiana with "propagation rights" there and in twenty other northern states from the Mississippi Valley to the Atlantic. In describing the extent of his northern empire, Stephenson would later say:

> I was assigned the job of organizing the klan in the state of Indiana. Thereafter other states were assigned. A na-

tional Department of Extension was organized and I was placed in charge, to organize the klan in the states of Indiana, Illinois, Iowa, Nebraska, Kansas, Missouri, Minnesota, Wisconsin, Kentucky, Tennessee, Ohio, Michigan, Pennsylvania, New Jersey, Connecticut, New Hampshire, Massachusetts, Vermont, Maine, Maryland and West Virginia.

. . . I established headquarters in the principal cities of these states, and opened a central office in Columbus, Ohio. The assignment of this territory was made in the late Fall of 1922 and the early Spring of 1923."[8]

He quickly set about a massive recruiting drive in his new dominions with all the zeal and organizational techniques of a master sales manager. In addition to the Klan's hundreds of rank-and-file Kleagles working on commission, he hired full-time, professional sales organizers, some of them stocks and bonds salesmen, some Florida real estate promoters.

In less than two years, by the age of thirty-three, he would amass a fortune of more than 3 million dollars, largely from his share of Klan membership fees and his sale of Klan robes and hoods in his northern realms. He would have a mansion in suburban Indianapolis, a fleet of Cadillacs, a $75,000 yacht on Lake Erie, a summer "White House" on Buckeye Lake in Ohio, and a private airplane with personal pilot.

Reports of Stephenson's share in Klan initiation fees vary. Some say he was keeping about four dollars out of every ten-dollar fee; others that the official Klan breakdown was four dollars for the Kleagle and one dollar for the King Kleagle, which Stephenson was before he became Grand Dragon. In any event, his income sources went far beyond Indiana, as he had propagation rights in many other states. Most agree that he made huge profits on Klan robes and hoods, having them manufactured for about $1.75 and selling them for around $6.00. Norman Weaver says he made even more money selling influence in politics and legislation, as in the 1924 elections and the 1925 session of the Indiana legislature.

He loved luxury and fast living. But his driving force, more potent than money, was power over people, the urge to organize and manipulate others. He devoured books on psychology and came to regard himself as a master mass psychologist. He also began writing a book on master salesmanship. Weaver said that "most estimates of his personality stress his ambition and overwhelming urge to wield power, to control people."[9]

One of his idols was Benito Mussolini, the fascist dictator who had taken power in Italy. Writing in the *New Republic* in 1927, Alva W. Taylor said, "like his illustrious mentor, Mussolini, he turned from Socialism to a crusade against the 'Reds'. . . . Mussolini's methods were to his mind the model for men of action like himself."[10] (Mussolini was also once popular with Klan orators down the line for more ideological reasons. Essentially, they saw his break with the Vatican as a defense against Catholicism. Later, when Il Duce patched up his differences with the Holy See, they discarded him as "just another Italian.")

Booth, in a clearly anti-Stephenson book, said that in 1922 Stephenson thought the stage was set for a "revolution" in the United States. He was determined to be the Mussolini who arose from the chaos and mob violence to take control of the government.[11] This was most probably anti-Stephenson overkill. Yet, by 1924 Stephenson had his eye on a U.S. Senate seat, with hopes that it would lead to the 1928 Republican nomination for president.

(Senator Samuel M. Ralston, elected in 1922 with Klan support even before Stephenson's rise to full power, was ailing in 1924 and not expected to live out his term. He died in October 1925, but by that time Stephenson was on trial for murder. Governor Jackson appointed Arthur R. Robinson to fill the vacancy.)

To organize his new northern dominions, Stephenson first set up office in Columbus, Ohio. Later, in 1923, he moved his headquarters to downtown Indianapolis, an eight-room suite taking up the entire third floor of the Kresge Building at Washington and Pennsylvania streets.

It was nominally the headquarters of his coal business, known as the Central States Coal Company. But from here, through an intelligence network that reached into every county and town, he would soon be sending out the word that would make or break candidates for public office—state legislators, mayors, sheriffs, school board members, city council members.

The casing of the door to his private office bore the inscription, "The bearers of evil tidings shall be slain." Inside, visitors found him sitting beside a huge American flag, a bronze bust of Napoleon, and a battery of eight telephones. Despite his comparative youth, he liked to refer to himself in messages to subordinates as "The Old Man." But to his associates and many of his admirers he was known simply as "Steve."

His charisma spread rapidly throughout the Middle West, through his speeches, Klan publications, and word of mouth. His private plane enabled him to move rapidly from place to place to rally Klan organizers. He loved speaking and managed to hold audiences through long hours. Booth said that "in Indianapolis early in 1923 he spoke to about 500 Ku Klux Klan workers from nine o'clock in the morning until about three in the afternoon," stopping only briefly "for a cup of coffee while his listeners had sandwiches and doughnuts." Another time, in Springfield, Illinois, "he spoke for four hours without a stop, and in Ohio he delivered an address which started about one o'clock in the afternoon and lasted until after seven. Not one person left until he had finished."[12]

His influence went far beyond the sites of his personal appearances. As the symbol of a new crusade, his reputation spread over literally hundreds of thousands of northern Klansmen in Pennsylvania, Ohio, Illinois, Wisconsin, Michigan, Iowa, and Colorado and even pervaded California. Strangely his fame had apparently not reached his parents in Oklahoma. His father, Arizona Stephenson, died in 1923 at the age of seventy four, but Stephenson, said Booth, was unaware of it as "his family had lost all trace of him."

In summer 1923, Stephenson conceived the idea of establishing what some newspapers called a "Klan Kollege." Indiana's Valparaiso University, a small but respected institution, was facing financial problems. Stephenson would have the Klan buy it up and make it a school for the children of Klansmen. Imperial Wizard Evans refused to put up money. More importantly, the purchase was never seriously considered by the university itself. Nevertheless, rumors persisted that the Klan had taken it over, or would soon do so.

Finally, in early 1924, Valparaiso president Horace M. Evans and a committee of distinguished former students issued a public denial, declaring the university "open to the education of all without thought of race, religion, social standing, wealth, politics, or influence." They said a new code adopted by the school's trustees "proclaims opposition to any individual, group, lodge, church or society which intentionally endeavors to separate our people into class-conscious groups, setting one against the other in promotion of hatred."

"This pronouncement," they continued, "is taken as a vigorous stand against the Ku Klux Klan and to mean that henceforth as heretofore, Valparaiso University cannot be named as an educational institution controlled by any class, organization or any religious sect."[13]

By now, though few were aware of it, certain patterns of deceit had appeared. His use of the title "The Old Man" instead of his name in his communications had been a simple act of dissembling, apparently to cast an aura of mysticism about himself that would appeal to the Klan mind's love of secrecy. Insiders knew it was Stephenson, but outsiders might not. ("The Old Man" was also a sort of affectionate title sometimes used by soldiers for a commanding officer.)

But, at the same time, he had never tried to dispel the myth that he had fought as a major in France. And of the eight telephones in his Indianapolis office, one was a fake through which he pretended to receive calls from the White House and other high places to impress gullible visitors. At his coronation in Kokomo in 1923, he reportedly apologized for being late, saying he had been "kept unduly long" in consultation with the president of the United States.

A magazine reporter who interviewed him in 1924 said he appeared "decisive and energetic," but then added: "Strangely enough, the eyes fail to carry the conviction of sincerity. They do not sparkle. They observe, study, impress one with expedience, as their owner 'sells himself' to his prospect. Beneath what is intended as disarming frankness, stratagem obviously lurks."[14]

John Niblack, an Indianapolis judge who once worked as a reporter for the *Indianapolis Times*, recalls an incident when Stephenson seemed to show symptoms of slight mental disturbance. As a young reporter he visited Stephenson's Indianapolis office one day and walked over beside a large plate-glass window. Stephenson appeared alarmed and told him to get away from the window. "There are people lying over there in the point of the Indiana Trust Building with high-powered rifles just trying to shoot me," he said, "and they might shoot you by mistake." Niblack later went over to the Indiana Trust Building and found no sign of rifles; quite the contrary, two of the offices facing Stephenson's suite were occupied by attorneys for the Klan.

"I concluded," Niblack said, "that Stephenson must be suffering hallucinations. In fact, after I knew him pretty well I decided he was a slight mental case, which by no means dimmed his brilliance of thought. He certainly had a lot of the two main symptoms of *dementia praecox*, illusions of grandeur and delusions of persecution."[15] By 1924 an anti-Stephenson faction encouraged by Evans was becoming active in the Indiana Klan, but there is no evidence that an assassination was planned. Later, however, during his murder trial in Noblesville, there were reported threats on his life.

Beneath the surface deceits and stratagems lay an even darker side of Stephenson, a pattern of alcohol and impulsive sexual behavior that would eventually lead to the state prison, but that also was yet to be revealed to his multitude of admirers. Certainly none of this was in the minds of the thousands of Klansmen and their families who flooded into Kokomo on the Fourth of July, 1923, to attend the Klan's Indiana charter convention[16] and to see their hero crowned Grand Dragon of the new Indiana realm, or Klan state organization.

They came from every county in Indiana and several surrounding states in a special train, by interurban railway, and in thousands of automobiles. Klan estimates of the throng, probably exaggerated, ranged up to 200,000. Whatever the total it was surely the biggest northern gathering in Klan history, and it engulfed Kokomo—a city of 30,000 about fifty miles north of Indianapolis—like an invading army. They were accompanied by thirty bands, some to play, most only to march with a slow roll of drums in a night parade that stretched for miles. They brought food, camping gear, and children dressed in little Klan outfits.

Robert Coughlan, a one-time *Life* editor who grew up in Kokomo, was then a boy of nine. He recalls the scene as he rode with his family out toward Melfalfa Park, a state Klan retreat west of the city and the site of Stephenson's coronation. The Coughlans were not Klansmen; on the contrary, they were Roman Catholics and had gone out of sheer curiosity, only after Coughlan's mother's initial worries had been overcome.

> We saw white-sheeted Klansmen everywhere. They were driving along the streets, walking about with their hoods thrown back, eating in restaurants—they had taken the town over. But it was not until we were well out toward Melfalfa Park that we could realize the size of the demonstration. The road was a creeping mass of cars. They were draped with flags and bunting and some carried homemade signs with slogans such as "America for the Americans" or

"The Pope will sit in the White House when Hell freezes over." There were Klan traffic officials every few yards, on foot, on motorcycle, on horseback . . . the air was full of the noise of their police whistles and shouts. The traffic would congeal, grind ahead, stop again while the Klan families sat steaming and fanning themselves in their cars. Most of them seemed to have made it a real family expedition; the cars were loaded with luggage, camping equipment, and children. Quite a few of the latter—even those too young to belong to the junior order of the Klan—were dressed in little Klan outfits.[17]

Because of the crush the Coughlan family turned off on a side road before they reached the park. In any case, they would not have been admitted without special credentials or a secret password. But from eyewitnesses and copious newspaper accounts, Coughlan and others have reconstructed a scene unparalleled in Indiana history. The ceremonies began about 9:30 A.M., with a prayer by one V. W. Blair (the program printed in newspapers does not call him "Reverend"). Then a fifty-piece boys' band from New Castle, Indiana, played "The Star-Spangled Banner."

The Reverend Everett Nixon, Exalted Cyclops of the Kokomo Klan, gave a brief address of welcome. Then the national leader of the Klan—Dr. Hiram Wesley Evans from Atlanta—mounted the platform. He warned of "foreign influences" and urged Klansmen to vote for congressmen who would work for "rehabilitation" of the nation so that Americans could be "born into American heritage."

By lunchtime the central character—Stephenson—had still not arrived. Along Wildcat Creek the ladies of Klan auxiliary units had set up block-long cafeteria tables loaded with soda pop, near-beer, roast beef, and buns. Then about 2:00 P.M., with thousands of robed Klansmen and their families gathered in the park's meadows, a yellow airplane appeared in the sky to the south. Under its wings was painted: Evansville KKK No. 1. It slowly circled a flat open field and landed. To a surge of applause, "Steve," in a silken orange and purple robe, emerged from the rear

44

cockpit. A small cadre of Klan dignitaries escorted him to the speaker's platform. Steve raised his right hand to quiet the crowd. Many later accounts have quoted him as saying in effect:

> *My worthy subjects, citizens of the Invisible Empire, Klansmen all, greetings! It grieves me to be late. The President of the United States kept me unduly long counseling on vital matters of state. Only my plea that this is the time and place of my coronation obtained for me surcease from his prayers for guidance.*

> *Here in this uplifted hand where all can see I bear an official document, addressed to the Grand Dragon, Hydras, Great Titans, Furies, Giants, Kleagles, Empire of the Realm of Indiana . . . It is signed by his Lordship Hiram Wesley Evans, Imperial Wizard, and duly attested. It continues me officially in my exalted capacity as Grand Dragon of the Invisible Empire for the Realm of Indiana. It so proclaims me by Virtue of God's Unchanging Grace. So be it.*[19]

Whether he used these same words or not is open to question. Newspapers of the time don't mention them, but reporters had agreed to certain restrictions in order to gain admission to the Klan park. In any case, as Norman Weaver said, "The point is, the words fit. He *could* have said it, it fits his character."[18]

With no mention of Stephenson's reported prefatory remarks, and identifying him only as "the grand dragon of the realm of Indiana," the *Kokomo Dispatch* of July 5, 1923, published extensive excerpts from his "Back to the Constitution" speech—probably from a text distributed to the press. In them one finds nothing of the anti-Catholic, anti-Semitic, WASP-racist, supremacy appeals used by Klan organizers down the line. But he was still telling his middle western populist audience what they wanted to hear: The Constitution gave power to the people, but this principle has been distorted by spoils politicians, big money interests, and the courts that support them. If the founders were alive today, "they would correct the subsequent political perversions of some of its most sacred and fundamental provisions by rewriting those provisions so simply and specifically that no enemy of representative government could any longer, or ever again, distort or evade them." They would also write into the Constitution such new features as "changing conditions have made essential to the common welfare and high destiny of this republic" so that "not even a supreme court could fail to comprehend exactly their meaning and relation to the common welfare."

He called for direct power for Congress to override the Supreme Court. He said he believed the founders would "make it possible for Congress by a two-thirds or three-fourths vote to pass a law over the judicial vote." He also said that "no Supreme Court decision as to the constitutionality of a federal enactment should be at all binding" by a mere majority vote. It should require a vote of at least seven of the nine members.

In any case, he called for direct power for Congress to over-ride the Supreme Court. He said he believed the founders would "make it possible for Congress by a two-thirds or three-fourths vote to pass a law over the judicial vote." Finally, beyond Congress, he called for a popular vote on court decisions. With a fine disregard for the founders' concerns about unrestrained mass rule, he said, "I believe that the forefathers would today provide that any adverse decision affecting the validity of the Constitution might be submitted to a referendum of the sovereign people, whose basic fundamental law it is."

Wall Street and big money vested interests were then favorite targets of increasingly hard-pressed middle western farmers. Stephenson knew he would find ready ears far beyond his Klan audience when he said: "The Constitution gave Congress the power to coin money and regulate the value thereof." But now, "there is private, not public, control of currency and credit. The power over the value of money is not exercised by Congress as the fathers intended.

It is in the hands of selfishly interested individuals, usually working as a class."

Although Stephenson was not identified by name, one might guess he was already laying the groundwork for the day he thought he could emerge as a national populist leader—even a dictator—and that he had directed that copies of his speech be distributed to the press. In its issue of July 6, 1923, the *Fiery Cross* published the speech in full, but still identified Stephenson only as "The Old Man" and in a lengthy prefatory headline called his performance a "Stirring Address" by a man "Beloved of all Klansmen" which was "Received Amidst Remarkable and Inspiring Demonstration."

Some accounts of Stephenson's coronation say that as he finished speaking the crowd showered him with money, rings, watch charms, and other tributes. Niblack, who covered the affair for the *Indianapolis Times* and sat near Stephenson as he spoke, said he never saw this, at least on the speaker's platform.

In its story of July 5, 1923, the *Kokomo Daily Tribune* says only that, when the selection of the Grand Dragon was announced, just before Stephenson began speaking, "the individual chosen was given an ovation and presented with a gold medal and a cross set with jewels, a gift of all Hoosier Klansmen."

Interestingly enough, there is no mention of Stephenson's name in any of the stories about the rally in the Indiana newspapers that covered it. On the day before the rally, July 3, 1923, a Klan program printed on the *Kokomo Tribune*'s front page lists his scheduled speech only as "An address by 'The Old Man' on 'Back to the Constitution.'" A man who spoke on "The Legal Justification of the Klan" was listed only as "The Best Lawyer in Indiana."

Reporters, to gain admittance to the Klan property, had agreed to certain confidences. As the correspondent for the *Indianapolis Star* explained in his story the following day, "This is the first time that newspaper reporters not members of the organization have ever been permitted inside the inclosure [Melfalfa Park]. Under the provision it was necessary that the reporter in accepting the card [of admission] pledge 'on his word of honor and his newspaper integrity not to reveal the names of the speakers, individuals, participants or attendants at the meeting.'

"It is permitted, however, to use the names of those members of the imperial body whose names have become public through other channels. Chief among these was Dr. H. W. Evans, imperial wizard of Atlanta, Ga." Stephenson, whose name would within a year be spread across many a front page as he dominated Indiana politics, was still part of a shadow world.

The actual size of the crowd in Melfalfa Park that day is still a matter of conjecture. The *Indianapolis Star* of July 5 said that the official checker at the main gate, where it was necessary to show press badges or whisper the password in order to gain admittance, reported that up to the close of the afternoon he had counted slightly more than fifty-thousand automobiles that had either parked inside the forty-acre tract or driven up to discharge passengers.

Earlier in the day, from his seat at the press table near where Stephenson spoke, Niblack said he estimated the crowd assembled to hear the Grand Dragon at about ten thousand. Robert Coughlan, who followed up his childhood memories with additional research, concluded, however, that the total in Kokomo that day—including Klansmen and their families from Indiana, Ohio, and Illinois—may indeed have come close to the Klan claim of nearly 200,000 as reported in the *Fiery Cross*.

Allen Safianow, professor of history at the University of Indiana at Kokomo, has concluded that all of the crowd estimates are "subject to question," and also indicates that the size of the crowd *vis-à-vis* Kokomo's normal population could lead to exaggerations in the memories of those who were there. "There is no way to determine the precise size of the crowd that gathered in Kokomo that hot July Fourth," he wrote. "Local residents who recall the day remain impressed with the throngs that flocked to town.

Nonetheless, a crowd considerably under the 200,000 figure reported by the Klan publication the *Fiery Cross* would seem tremendous to a population of 30,000."[20] He also questions the claim that the Kokomo rally was the largest or one of the largest Klan gatherings ever held in America. A 1925 homecoming celebration for Imperial Wizard Evans in Texas may have surpassed this, though it included many gathered at a state fair.

The figure of fifty thousand cars arriving at Melfalfa Park in one day also seems highly improbable. This could have been a typographical error or misquotation, with the gate checker actually reporting slightly more than five thousand.

Nevertheless, all agree that the throng was the biggest that ever converged on Kokomo, and the largest ever assembled by the Klan in its northern realms. To the newly certified Grand Dragon, the one-time tramp printer turned master salesman, the applause of thousands signalled the way to even more wealth and power. It must also have seemed a tribute to his ability to manipulate people. But salesmanship alone could never have done it. Beneath the cheers lay prejudices and fears with deep roots in American life.

3

Target: Rome

IN THE MAMMOTH Fourth of July parade that followed Stephenson's Kokomo triumph of 1923, one center of attraction was a huge American flag stretched horizontally almost from curb to curb and carried by a dozen men on each side. As the flag passed by, the Klan crowds showered it with bills and coins, shouting "Throw in! Give to the hospital!"

The money, as proclaimed, was to go into a building fund for a new Kokomo hospital. Earlier in the day a Klan refreshment stand in Melfalfa Park had made a similar appeal with a huge sign: "No change given. All proceeds go to the Howard County Hospital."

Such charities were not an uncommon Klan practice, but behind this one lay a special enthusiasm. The only Kokomo hospital then was the Good Samaritan, a Catholic institution operated by the Sisters of Saint Joseph. The new hospital, as Klansmen told one another, would be *non-Catholic*, a Klan-approved hospital that would keep loyal Americans out of the hands of the agents of Rome.

Though the hospital fund drive was underway locally before the Klan rally, and though the new hospital was still some years away, the flag and the money symbolized what was then the Invisible Empire's strongest appeal in Indiana and many other states: a fearful Protestant-nativist patriotism turned into a paranoid anti-Catholicism; a belief that anyone loyal to the Pope of Rome could not be fully loyal to America; a widespread apprehension that Rome was out to take over the United States.

The Roman Catholic population of Indiana then numbered less than 10 percent of the state's nearly three million people. But, like the suspected and real Communists of the McCarthy era, they—or more specifically their Pope and his Roman establishment—were seen by many as an imminent peril to the American Way of Life.

In pursuing the reasons why people joined the Klan, John Mecklin found that "the motive which has gained the most members—taking precedence over all others in the strength and universality of its appeal, is undoubtedly anti-Catholicism. . . . Furthermore, it is insisted that this anti-Catholicism is not to be identified with mere religious prejudice. Klansmen reiterate that they are not opposed to Catholicism as a religion." Deeper than differences in ritual, he said, "lies the vague feeling that the center of authority of the Roman Catholic Church, as opposed to Protestantism, lies outside of and superior to the American society in which Catholics and Protestants live. The Klan interprets this as a menace to the spiritual and moral integrity of America."[1]

The Klan did not invent anti-Catholicism. It was a syndrome that lay deep in Anglo-Saxon culture, going back to the split of England's King Henry VIII from the Pope in the early 1500s. An anti-Romanist mind-set had arrived with the first settlers of Jamestown, Virginia, in 1607, fresh from an antipapist, Protestant-Reformed England where the political and civil liberties of Catholics were severely restricted, including denial of the right to vote or hold public office; where the defeat of a menacing Catholic Spanish Armada in 1588 was still a vivid memory.

Here it would alternately smolder and flare over more

than three centuries before it erupted in the Ku Klux Klan phenomenon of the 1920s. The Klan was, in fact, in many ways a revival of the nativist Know-Nothing movement of the 1850s, which had urged denial of public office to Catholics and foreigners and a twenty-one-year residence for immigrants before they could become naturalized and vote.

Beyond the absurd myths spread by Klan propagandists, many Americans, both in and out of the Invisible Empire, continued to raise what seemed to be logical and troubling questions:

Could a church that had historically stood for union of church and state really support a strict separation of church and state, as specified in the United States Constitution?

Could a church that censored the speech, writings, and even the reading of its members to make them conform with its interpretations of church doctrines fully support the American principles of free speech and press? (Though the Klan never seems to have made a specific issue of it, an index of forbidden books issued by Rome had proscribed Catholics from reading the works of more than 130 authors, including Zola, Balzac, Heine, Maeterlinck, and Hume, along with Gibbon's *Decline and Fall of the Roman Empire*.[2])

Would not Catholics in Congress and state legislatures follow the Pope's policies rather than the broader public interest in their votes on public issues?

Others insisted that the church was adaptable to its environment. Henry Steele Commager said:

Logically, some Catholic doctrines spelled hostility to some of the principles and institutions which America cherished. ... The Catholic Church was one of the most logical human institutions. But its logic, unlike that of communism, rejected the doctrinaire approach and adapted itself to realities. These [church] doctrines, Catholic apologists explained, applied only to some ideal situation or to some country completely Catholic and had no present relevance to the United States.[3]

Relevant or irrelevant, anti-Catholic propagandists could always dredge up atrocious examples of Catholic persecutions from history: the Spanish Inquisition, the Saint Bartholomew's Day Massacre in Paris in 1572, the wholesale executions of Protestant heretics by English Catholic royalty. Nearly three hundred burned at the stake in the "fires of Smithfield" during a short-lived resurgence of Catholic power from 1553 to 1558 under Queen "Bloody Mary" Tudor I.

At a more primitive, titillating level, stories of licentiousness among priests could always be fabricated, and lent credence by isolated periods of corruption in church history, as in the profligate sex lives of the Borgias and a Catholic cardinal who had five illegitimate children before he became Pope Alexander VI (1492–1503).

As Robert Coughlan wrote, "the Borgias were [to the Klan] an endless source of material, and their exploits came to be as familiar to readers of the Klan press as the lives of soap opera characters are to modern housewives. Constant readers must have begun to think of them as the typical Catholic family of the Renaissance."[4]

Fed by the Klan propaganda, many people were ready to believe almost any story about bishops, priests, and nuns. In their classic sociological study "Middletown"—actually Muncie, Indiana—Robert and Helen Lynd described what was probably not an untypical case in the mid-1920s:

"Lady," exclaimed one earnest woman to one of the staff interviewers, "you have asked me a lot of questions and now I want to ask you some. Do you belong to the Klan?" To a negative response she continued, "Well, it's about time you joined the other good people and did something about this Catholic situation. The Pope is trying to get control of this country, and in order to do it he started the old Klan to stir up trouble among the Protestants, but instead of doing it he only opened their eyes to the situation, and now all the Protestants are getting together in the new Klan to overcome the Catholic menace. I just want to show you here in this copy of *The Menace* [a Klan propaganda sheet]—look at this picture of this poor girl—look at her hands! See all those fingers gone—just stumps left! She was in a convent where it was considered sinful to wear jewelry and the Sisters, when they found her wearing some rings, just burned them off her fingers!"

In a footnote the Lynds report that the subject was a "neat, healthy-looking woman of thirty-seven, the mother of four children and wife of one of the highest grades of workers in an automobile plant. The husband earns $40.00 a week and had had no unemployment in five years; the family owns its home, though it is mortgaged, owns a new Ford sedan, and plans to send the oldest child to a local college."[5]

Though many residents today consider the story apocryphal, the antipapist frenzy was reported to have reached a peak in North Manchester, a small town in Wabash County. One evening, according to an oft-repeated account, a Klan orator had warned his audience that the Pope himself might then be in Indiana:

"He may be on the northbound train tomorrow," the speaker shouted. "Be warned! Prepare! America is for Americans! Watch the trains!"

Next day, so the story goes, several hundred people were assembled at the little railroad station watching for the northbound Monon for Chicago. It was not a busy passenger terminal and anyone detraining there was conspicuous. This day, a single passenger, a traveling salesman, got off only to be surrounded by a hostile crowd. It took him some time to convince them that he was not really Pius XI in disguise.[6]

Stories that Catholic churches across the nation were storing arms in their basements and that Catholic militia were secretly drilling at night were widely believed. So were macabre tales that when aging convents were being built or dismantled, workers had found the hidden corpses of infants—the product of illicit relations between priests and nuns. In Indianapolis, one movie including a short scene of Christopher Columbus unfurling the banners of Catholic Spain in the New World was denounced as Catholic propaganda.

One myth led to another. Soon it was reported—and widely believed—that the Pope was coming to Washington, D.C., to place himself personally at the head of an uprising against the United States. Photographs of the Protestant Episcopal Cathedral of Saints Peter and Paul on Washington's Mount Alban, then under construction, were passed around as pictures of what was to be the "new Vatican." According to the Klan, it was placed four-hundred feet above Washington so that field guns could be fired directly on the Capitol and White House.

It was, in part, a transfer of wartime fervor—and gullibility—into a new channel. The country had just come through a war in which many Americans really believed that German soldiers had skewered Belgian babies on bayonets and chained their own women to machine guns in the Argonne. Germany was defeated but the wartime fever lingered on. At the same time, the new high life of a postwar generation—bootleggers, teenage drinking, jazz, open adultery, midnight trysts in automobiles—had unnerved the small-town orthodox Protestant mind. Often the Klan got its first foothold as a force for morality and law and order.

In many Protestant churches it was not uncommon for a group of hooded Klansmen to appear in the middle of Sunday evening services, march to the altar, and deposit contributions of fifty dollars or more. Sometimes the minister then obligingly led his flock in singing "Onward Christian Soldiers" as the visitors departed.

New trends in modern thought—evolution, religious ecumenism, internationalism—also threatened long-standing fundamentalist and nationalist beliefs.

The reasoning that incorporated all of this with a crusade against the Roman Catholic church may seem difficult to follow, but it went something like this: What is happening is alien and un-American. The Catholic church is alien and un-American. Therefore, a 100 percent American crusade to rid a community of bootleggers and prostitutes and protect its children against dangerous new ideas must also be a crusade for America against the church of Rome.

The same Klansmen who raided bootleggers and patrolled lovers' lanes also spread slanderous rumors about goings-on between priests and nuns behind convent walls. One example of how far the Klan could go in lumping sin and Catholicism together was an Indiana recruiting appeal that read:

> Every criminal, every gambler, every thug, every libertine, every girl ruiner, every home wrecker, every wife-beater, every dope peddler, every moonshiner, every crooked politician, every pagan Papist priest, every shyster lawyer, every K. of C. [member of the Catholic Knights of Columbus], every white slaver, every brothel madam, every Rome-controlled newspaper, every black spider—is fighting the Klan. Think it over. Which side are you on?"[7]

Probably the Klan's most vicious attack on the Roman Catholic church came in its distribution through Indiana in 1924 of at least 100,000 copies of a purported oath the Klan said was taken by initiates into the Catholic Knights of Columbus:

> I do further promise and declare that I will . . . wage relentless war, secretly and openly, against all heretics, Protestants and Masons . . . and that I will hang, burn, waste, boil, flay, strangle and bury alive those infamous heretics . . . rip up the stomachs and wombs of their women, and crash their infants' heads against the walls in order to annihilate their inexecrable [sic] race.[8]

Racism, anti-Semitism, and antipathy toward foreigners in general surely played a part—along with anti-Catholicism—in the Klan's growth in the Middle West. The Indiana towns with their signs warning "Nigger, don't let the sun set on you here" were not the only threats. On one primary election day in Indianapolis, Klansmen paraded through black neighborhoods waving pistols. A Greek fruit merchant might have been threatened for planning to marry a "white woman." Jews were objects of suspicion, especially in financial affairs.

But as long as these people kept "in their place," they were only marginal concerns. They were, after all, not united and directed by an insidious foreign power like the Pope of Rome.

Morton Harrison, writing in the *Atlantic* in 1928, said:

It is a well-known fact that a man cannot be induced to fear the neighbor near whom he has lived many years in peace and harmony. The Stephenson sales plan took this fact into consideration. It was the secret of its success.

The [Klan] campaign was directed not against the little band of Negroes who lived together down along the river, worked for the white folks, kept a religious revival in continuous operation, and minded their own business, but against a mythical wave of black labor sweeping up from the South to work for a dollar a day, live in squalor and commit unspeakable offenses against the white people.

No one was urged to lynch Nick, the smiling and busy Greek confectioner whose ice-cream parlor was a high school students' meeting place, but a terrifying curse was hurled against an unnamed Greek in the next county who had put an American-born citizen out of business by cut-throat competition, and especially against remote masses of unassimilated aliens in large cities awaiting only a Lenin to show them how to abolish by force the institution of private property.

No voice was lifted against the peace of Solomon Stein, the industrious amiable clothier, model family man and perhaps faithful attendant, as a visitor, upon the service of the Presbyterian church, but the welkin rang with invective hurled eastward in the general direction of a Jewish ring of international bankers who started the war and were preparing to foreclose a mortgage on the world, bankrupting Henry Ford and others.

The Catholics were the hard problem. In most Indiana communities, there is but one Catholic parish. Catholic children are required by diocesan orders to attend Catholic schools. The families live near the church because their religious and educational interest is centered in it. The adults mingle socially but little with the Protestant people, the children less. The Catholic church ritual is so foreign to anything in the experience of the average American rural Protestant that a skilled agitator can ascribe to it many of the attributes of a pagan incantation. But the Catholics are important customers. Acting on the theory that the intensity of a weak man's hatred is measured directly in terms of his remoteness from his enemy, the Pope was selected as the arch-enemy of American purity. There are few things a Kokomo Klansman can do with greater safety than stand in the privacy of his own home and shake his fist at Rome, Italy.[9]

Some Protestants did, however, "mingle socially" with Catholic friends, whom they regarded not as enemies of America but simply people being misled. Robert Coughlan, the son of a Catholic public school teacher in Kokomo, recalled:

> Not all Catholics were in on the plot; for example the Catholics you knew. These were well-meaning dupes whom one might hope to save. . . . My parents were generally considered to be among them. My mother's friend, Mrs. Wilson, would come often and, in a high-strung and urgent manner, try to argue the thing out. Against my mother's gentle insistence to the contrary, she would usually end up by declaring "Now I want to tell *you*, honey! As sure as you're born, the Pope is coming over here with his shirt-tail aflyin'!"[10]

Meredith Nicholson, an Indianapolis writer who knew the Hoosier mind as well as anyone, said the Klan movement in Indiana seemed to be almost entirely anti-Catholic. But the same motivation went far beyond Indiana, as Mecklin found in his interviews with hundreds of Klansmen across the country. "All mentioned anti-Catholicism," he reported, "and a large percentage placed it first" among their reasons for joining.[11]

Catholics had long been a part of American life. The first permanent Catholic settlements in England's American colonies were made in Maryland in 1634. Here, especially under the proprietorship of Cecilius Calvert and dispensation from the British Crown, they enjoyed a few years of relative tolerance, but this was soon broken by religious strife, sparked at first by Virginia Anglicans. The church survived, but the colonial capital was moved from Catholic Saint Mary's to Protestant Annapolis.

At the time of the American Revolution, there were still only about thirty thousand Roman Catholics among some four million people in England's American colonies. A Maryland Catholic, Charles Carroll of Carrollton, was among the signers of the Declaration of Independence. Another Maryland Catholic, Daniel Carroll, and a Catholic from Pennsylvania, Thomas Fitzimons, were signers of the Constitution. But by the 1830s, new "native American" political leaders in New York would be urging that Catholics and foreigners be denied the right to vote or hold public office.

A new weekly newspaper called the *Protestant* was launched in January 1830 to warn Americans against the dangers of popery. Protestant preachers like Lyman Beecher began warning their flocks against Catholic imperialism. Samuel F. B. Morse, the pioneer telegrapher and father of the Morse Code, became a prolific writer of anti-Romanist tracts, and in 1834 produced a book called *Foreign Conspiracy against the Liberties of the United States*, warning against fantastic designs of the Church of Rome to take over much of America.

American public school children of the Nineteenth century were given heavy doses of anti-Catholicism in their textbooks. Ruth Miller Elson quotes one passage in a widely-used "general class book" which she says was typical: "For many ages the Popes not only considered themselves infallible, but exalted themselves above all the kings of the earth, to the very throne of CHRIST [caps sic]; assuming the right of pardoning sin, and of giving or rather selling the liberty of indulging in every species of wickedness and corruption."[12]

In many history books the Spanish Inquisition is described in lurid detail. One not untypical description of the persecutions tells the children: "The unhappy victims were either strangled or committed to the flames, or loaded with chains and shut up in dungeons . . . Nothing ever displayed so fully to the eyes of mankind the spirit and temper of the papal religion." In one school primer the pope is described as having deemed the burning of John Rogers, a Protestant martyr, in England and the St. Bartholomew's Day massacre in Paris "glorious events."[13]

As anti-Catholic feelings grew, some Americans themselves turned to violence. On August 11, 1834, the Ursuline Convent in Charlestown, Massachusetts, was burned to the ground. In 1844, armed clashes between Protestants and Catholics in Philadelphia left an estimated twenty people dead and one-hundred injured before the state militia was called in to suppress the disorders.

The impetus for all of this, as for later waves of nativism, was a fast-rising tide of immigration, much of it Catholic. In 1825, about 10,000 immigrants arrived. By 1835, this number grew to 45,374; in 1845, 114,371. From 1840 through 1850, the total U.S. population grew from 17,069,000 to 23,191,000—an increase of 6,122,000. Of this total increase, about 1,700,000—or more than 25 percent—were immigrants, almost 50 percent of them Irish Catholics, along with substantial numbers of German Catholics.

Popular emotions fused into new political movements: the Native American Association, which had originated in New York City in 1837; the American Republican party, also in New York, which opposed voting and office-holding rights for Catholics and foreigners and succeeded (with Whigs) in electing a nativist mayor; the American Republican Association, and the Native American Party, which took its name at a national nativist convention in Philadelphia in July 1845. Among other things, its platform called for changes in the naturalization laws, including an extended time before foreigners could be naturalized and vote.

The anti-Catholic and anti-immigrant movement of the

1840s flared again on a national scale in the 1850s. By 1854, it had become a national political force. Its formal title was the American party, but it was popularly called the Know-Nothing party because its members in various secret lodges replied "I know nothing" or "I don't know" when asked about their operations.

Know-Nothing goals included barring Catholics and foreigners from public office and mandating a twenty-one-year residence in the United States for immigrants before they could become naturalized and have voting privileges. In 1856, the Know-Nothings ran former President Millard Fillmore for another term in the White House. Fillmore came in a poor third behind James Buchanan and John C. Frémont, but still got more than 874,500 popular votes out of a total of about four million.

With their defeat in 1856, and with the nation preoccupied with the slavery issue and the gathering clouds of civil war, the Know-Nothings dwindled and finally disappeared in the war itself. But while the party disappeared, its spirit lived on. One historian of the Know-Nothing movement wrote that it was based on "the time-honored Anglo-Saxon and Evangelical aspersion of the integrity of Catholic citizenship, an aspersion as old as the age of Queen Elizabeth and responsible for the persecuting statutes of her time; an aspersion too, which though diminishing in force from generation to generation, is nevertheless likely to recur in years to come."[14] This was written long before the Klan phenomenon of the 1920s, but the historian could hardly have predicted the future more accurately.

Nativism notwithstanding, the Catholic population of the United States continued to grow. Overall, in the fifty years between 1815 and 1866, the church received an estimated 2,720,000 new members from abroad, Ireland accounting for most of them with about 1,683,000. At the same time, the natural increase of Catholic families already in America provided another 1,458,400.[15]

Meanwhile, a new—and, to many, threatening—centralization of authority in Rome had added to American nativist fears. In 1864, with new liberal and nationalist movements seeming to challenge his sovereignty, Pope Pius IX had issued his *Quanta Cura* and its accompanying *Syllabus of Errors*—denouncing, among other things, secularism, liberalism, and liberal Catholics' support of a "free church in a free state."[16]

It was an "error" he said, to place all religions on a par as the path to salvation, that is, to say that one was as good as another. It was also an error to consider the state as the origin of all rights; an error to think that civil law must prevail in conflicts between church and state. Many Americans saw this as an indictment of their society and a threat to their principle of separation of church and state.

Fears grew anew when in 1870 the First Vatican Council proclaimed the infallibility of the pope, according to the wishes of Pius IX. Under this doctrine, the pope, as head of the universal church, has authority to give definitive judgment on questions of faith and morals. Because he had divine guidance, he could not be in error.

With new tides of immigration and this new authoritarian tone from Rome, the stage was set by the 1880s for the immediate predecessor of the 1920s Ku Klux Klan: the American Protective Association (APA), one of the most rabidly anti-Catholic movements in American history.

The APA was founded in 1887 in Clinton, Iowa, by Henry F. Bowers. It was soon taken over by a shrewd political activist from Michigan named William J. Traynor. By 1892, it had about seventy thousand members in the Upper Mississippi Valley. By 1896, it claimed more than 2 million and had established its own magazine and some seventy weekly newspapers.

Like the Klan, the APA flourished in rural and small-town America rather than large metropolitan areas where Catholics were concentrated. Also like the Klan, it spread outrageous rumors and lies, such as that of a encyclical that purportedly set a time for Catholics to rise up and slay fellow Americans in a holy massacre. It became a political force, swinging elections in 1894 in Ohio, Wisconsin, Indiana, Missouri, and Michigan.

One factor in its phenomenal growth was the financial panic of 1893, when nearly five hundred banks and more than fifteen thousand businesses failed. The panic was sparked by the failure of a British banking house—Baring Brothers—and the sudden unloading of American securities by British investors, but the APA blamed it on a papal plot.

More impelling for the APA, however, was the growth of the Catholic population in America and especially the spread of Catholic parochial schools, where it was feared children would be indoctrinated with "un-American" principles.

Between 1870 and 1900, the Catholic population of the United States increased from 4,504,000 to 12,041,000. The biggest factor was the natural growth of Catholic families already here, an increase of 4,178,000. Immigration was next (3,079,000), and conversions (estimated at 280,000) during the same period.[17] In 1840, nativist fears had been stirred when only one out of seventeen Americans was a Roman Catholic. By 1895, the figure was one in six.

This growth could hardly be displeasing to the leaders of the Catholic church. Even as diplomatic a prelate as Cardinal James Gibbons of Baltimore said, "The birth rate in the United States is all in favor of the church. The Irish, the Catholic Germans and Canadians are proverbially prolific; and there are other reasons which we may not enter on here, and which point to an entirely disproportionate increase of Catholics in the near future."[18]

Cardinal Gibbons, an enlightened and dedicated American, was never accused of trying to take over America. But the pope's appointment in 1892 of an Italian archbishop, Francesco Satolli, as the apostolic delegate of the Vatican to the United States was something else. He was seen by the APA and its supporters as clear evidence of a Roman invasion.

Satolli's 1893 address to students of Gonzaga College, a

Jesuit school in Spokane, Washington, did little to change this image. "The action of the Catholic faith and morality is favorable in every way to the direction in which the Constitution turns," he said. "The more public opinion and government favor the Catholic schools, the more will the welfare of the commonwealth be advanced. The Catholic education is the surest safeguard of the permanence through the centuries of the Constitution and the best guide of the Republic in civic progress. From this source the Constitution will gather that assimilation so necessary for the perfect organization of the great progressive body which is the American Republic."[19]

Wittingly or unwittingly, he had exacerbated an issue as deep and as old as the nativist movements of the 1840s: public financial support for Catholic parochial schools, the very channel through which many nativists feared Rome would eventually take over America. As early as 1843, Catholic efforts to get public funds for their schools in New York State had brought on a nativist movement to restrict their voting privileges. The APA and its backers could quickly use Satolli's words as proof that the pope planned to transform America into a Catholic nation.

The address aroused widespread opposition not only among Protestants, but among American Catholic leaders as well. One of the most outspoken was Bishop John Spalding of Peoria, Illinois, a leading Catholic educator and one of the founders of the Catholic University of America in Washington, D.C.

> That the Delegate Satolli has been and is a source of strength to the Apaists [members of the APA], Bishop Spalding said, "... there can be no doubt Anti-Catholic prejudice is largely anti-papal prejudice; and when the organs of public opinion were filled with the sayings and doings of 'the American pope' who though a foreigner, with no intentions of becoming a citizen, ignorant alike of our language and traditions, was supposed to have supreme authority in the Church of America, fresh fuel was thrown upon the fire of bigotry. The fact that his authority is ecclesiastical merely

and concerns Catholics not as citizens but as members of the Church is lost sight of by the multitudes who are persuaded that the papacy is a political power eager to extend its control wherever opportunity may offer.[20]

Bishop Spalding himself had long advocated that Catholics support their own schools, without public funding, and in a speech at the founding of the Catholic University of America, had spoken long in praise of the American political system and its separation of church and state.

By 1896, the APA was dying out. Internal dissensions—a disagreement over William McKinley in the presidential election and efforts by some leaders to form a third party, and arguments among the Scotch-Irish, Scandinavians, and nativists—had taken their toll. The APA survived in name until 1911, with Bowers coming back into control, but it had virtually disappeared as a political force.

However, like the mentality of the Know-Nothings, the spirit of the APA lived on. Unfortunately the work of more liberal Catholic leaders like Bishop Spalding and Bishops (later Archbishops) John Ireland of St. Paul, Minnesota, and John J. Keane,[21] first rector of the Catholic University of America—who had urged rapid "Americanization" of Catholic immigrants—had not erased fears that Rome was out to take over America.

Neither had the words of Gibbons in his speech at Rome when he became a cardinal in 1887:

> I say with a feeling of profound gratitude that I belong to a country where the civil government extends over us the aegis of protection without interfering with the legitimate exercise of our mission as ministers of the gospel of Christ. . . . American Catholics rejoice in our separation of church and state; and I can conceive of no combination of circumstances likely to arise which would make a union desirable either to church or state.[22]

How many Americans were reassured by his address, if they heard of it, cannot be known, but by the 1920s, in the flag-waving fever left over from World War I, fears of Roman

Catholicism as treason would flare again in the hoods, robes, and blazing crosses of the Ku Klux Klan.

When Grand Dragon Stephenson made his favorite speeches on "pure Americanism" and "back to the Constitution," he didn't have to mention Rome or the Pope as the enemies, or even believe that they were.

Others down the line were doing this for him.

4

Growth: The Visible-Invisible Empire

THEY CALLED THEMSELVES the Knights of the Invisible Empire. Their hooded faces were invisible in parades. Their membership lists were secret. One was often uncertain whether a next-door neighbor was a Klansman or not.

In public places they often approached one another with cautious acronyms: AYAK (Are you a Klansman)? AKIA (A Klansman I am). KIGY (Klansman I greet you). Then sometimes, SANBOG (Strangers are near; be on guard).

But to grow they also had to be visible—often spectacularly so. Their burning crosses could be seen a mile away. Their picnics and rallies were advertised and open to all. Public speakers, sometimes hired, sometimes volunteer, openly proclaimed the Klan gospel.

The opening of a Klan recruiting drive in a given area often included a public rally and a parade. Typical was one in Noblesville, a town of about five thousand some twenty miles north of Indianapolis, on the Saturday night of January 27, 1923—reported in the Klan's *Fiery Cross* weekly newspaper as the Invisible Empire's "first public appearance" in that community.[1]

The evening began with a Klan rally in the Knights of Pythias Armory. The principal speaker was the Reverend

A. H. Monroe, pastor of the Noblesville Christian Church, who extolled the virtues of 100 percent Americanism and the separation of church and state. Meanwhile, on the southeast corner of the courthouse yard (the courthouse where D. C. Stephenson would later be convicted of murder), an eighteen-foot-high cross, with a ten-foot cross arm, wrapped in burlap and soaked in kerosene, was erected. Curious spectators soon began lining the announced parade route.

The procession that followed was headed by a color bearer carrying a large American flag. Behind him came the Lebanon (Indiana) Drum Corps, beating a steady rhythm for the marchers. (There was no instrumental music in such Klan parades; sometimes only the slow beating of drums, sometimes complete silence.) Behind these came another, much larger, American flag carried by six robed Klansmen, one holding each corner and one holding the center of each side. They were followed by an open automobile carrying a cross with red, white, and blue battery-powered lights.

Then came the main body of white-robed, hooded Klansmen, more than two hundred strong, all wearing black gloves and with arms folded. Most of them, as later discovered, were not from Noblesville, but were out-of-towners brought in by the Kleagles to help get things started. Soon the cross was set ablaze. As they completed the parade, the white-sheeted figures gathered in its glow, while curious hundreds stood watching from the shadows just beyond.

Throughout 1922 and 1923 such displays attracted widespread attention and thousands of new members. As membership grew, the parades grew bigger. There was never a problem with a parade permit. Often the police chief himself was a Klansman or a Klan supporter. More important, there was little or no public controversy over letting the Klan parade. The time when Klan parades would be met by outraged counterdemonstrators was still far away.

Behind it all lay the master-salesman, showman's hand of D. C. Stephenson, who had a sure instinct for getting attention and followers. Some organizations seek publicity by sending newspapers press releases, which, if printed at all, often are relegated to obscure corners of inside pages. Stephenson made the news in the first place.

His Klan sales crews were instructed in detail on the burning of crosses. He knew the spectacle would give a thrill to would-be Klansmen and could hardly escape newspaper notice. Cross burning was not always accompanied by a rally or parade; sometimes a cross was burned on a hill near a town with only the local Kleagle on hand to touch the match. During Klan parades, hooded figures took control of nearby roads to redirect automobile traffic. Sometimes, however, this was done when there was not a Klan event within twenty miles, but only to impress drivers with the Klan presence.

On July 6, 1923, the Klan's *Fiery Cross* advertised an upcoming homecoming celebration and picnic to be given in Evansville's Mesker Park on July 14 "under auspices of the Knights of the Ku Klux Klan." The ad stated: "White Gentile Protestant People of Indiana and the Tri-State Territory are Cordially Invited." A "Klan Day" was promoted for the Indiana State Fair. In Fort Wayne, the Klan announced a Labor Day picnic, and invited the public. At such outings the Klan distributed its recruiting leaflets and got many, if not most, of its new members.

Children were not overlooked. Special events were often arranged for their benefit, like the picnic of the Marion County Junior Ku Klux Klan held in Hiawatha Gardens on the east side of Indianapolis in August 1924. The Klan *Kourier*, a publication widely circulated among church groups, sponsored an essay contest for children with Americanism its theme. Each issue also included a "Klan Kiddie Korner" with activities for younger children.

Public gatherings, pulpits, and even high school graduations, became platforms for Klan orators. At one graduation ceremony in Kokomo, the Reverend P. E. Greenwalt of the South Main Street Methodist Church climaxed his baccalaureate sermon on patriotism and clean living by whipping a homemade Klan flag out of his pocket.[2]

While the Klan fed on fears of the Pope of Rome, it often began in various areas by projecting an image of a sort of service club for community improvement. One organizing principle enunciated by Imperial Wizard Simmons and Grand Dragon Stephenson was: First find out what a particular community's pressing concerns and needs are—from cleaning up crime and political corruption to building new schools or hospitals—then promise to do—and do—something about them. In one set of "Field Regulations" issued to Klan units down the line, Stephenson ordered that each group periodically establish "a program in which one outstanding thing for the betterment of the community will be accomplished" (see Chapter 5, pp. 92–93).

In Muncie, the Klan was originally encouraged by businessmen fighting a corrupt political machine, but soon it was off on the same antipapist propaganda as the other Klan groups. One pro-Klan minister told his flock: "They say the Pope isn't wanted in Italy. France has been approached and she doesn't want him. The Balkans say no; Russia, 'not on your life!' England, Germany, Switzerland, Japan—all refuse." Then—reinforcing the myth that the Protestant-Episcopal Cathedral then under construction in Washington, D.C., was to be a "new Vatican," he added, "And they say the Catholics are building a great cathedral in our national capital in Washington which is to become his home." Then, as if half-ashamed at relaying this ridiculous rumor, he added, "I don't know this . . . but that's what they say."[3]

Many speakers tried to dispel impressions that the Klan was against certain ethnic groups or creeds. At one Muncie rally, a Klan lawyer from Indianapolis said: "We are charged with being against the Jew. We are against no man. Jesus Christ is the leader of the Klan. The Jew is not for him, and therefore the Jew has shut himself out of the Klan. We are not against the Negro. [But] Rome fell because she mixed her blood. God Almighty has commanded us 'thou shalt not mix thy blood' [through racial intermarriage.]"[4]

The Visible-Invisible Empire

On December 29, 1923, the Reverend Alfred A. Fletcher of Tipton, Indiana, came to the Baptist church in the little town of Hope to give a lecture entitled "The Beast and His Image vs. The Invisible Empire." After telling an overflow crowd that "you have to be 100 percent Christian to be 100 percent American," he said, "The Klan is not against the Roman church" but "against Roman political machinations." It is "not against the Negro," but only helping him to be a "better American."[5]

Still, "foreigners" were not to be trusted with full citizenship. At some Klan rallies the speakers called for delaying voting privileges of newly naturalized immigrants for twenty-one years: "We make our boys and girls live here twenty-one years before we allow them to vote," one said, "and we ought to do the same with all foreigners." He also attacked Catholic parochial schools. "Lincoln said that no nation can live half-slave and half-free. My friends, this nation cannot exist with half its children in the great American free school system and the other half being taught a different thing in the parochial schools."[6]

In the wake of picnics, parades, flaming crosses and rhetoric, with patriotism and moral fervor running high, Klan recruiting thrived. At the suggestion of an anonymous acquaintance, one might receive a membership application in the mail, or approached directly by a Kleagle. Or he might be invited personally by a friend to attend a Klan initiation ceremony. Once a man joined he was sometimes followed by his wife in a Klan ladies auxiliary, like the Kamelias or Queens of the Golden Mask, and by his children in the Junior Klans.

Those who paid their ten-dollar fee to be "naturalized" in a Klan initiation ceremony found little in that ritual that most law-abiding citizens could object to. There were no calls for night riding or violence, no open incitement of racial or religious hatreds.

The initiate—already certified as a native-born, Protestant American—would kneel in prayer in some Klan Klav-

71

ern lodge room or in a clearing in the woods, surrounded by men in white robes. He would pledge to preserve the rights and privileges of free public schools, free speech, free press, separation of church and state, and just laws against all enemies. Through 1922 and 1923 hundreds of thousands went through such a ritual.

When they set out to organize a community, the Klan Kleagles usually went first to find a few influential persons—often pastors of established Protestant churches, or more often members of the local Masonic lodge—known to be favorable to the Invisible Empire. They presented the Klan as a needed force for community uplift and as a guardian against real or perceived immorality.

These small groups became the nucleus for further growth, but among the masses recruited into the Klan's rank-and-file, few—if any, at first—were people of high professional or economic standing. In the beginning, many spectators at Klan parades encouraged each other to "watch the shoes." One couldn't see faces or clothing beneath the hoods and robes, but shoes could reveal social or economic status. There were few fine Florsheims or polished cordovans, but mostly the cheaper, more ordinary footgear then identified with the working classes.

Still, they were a majority and the Klan offered them an opportunity to be something special. As Morton Harrison wrote:

> Many Klansmen lacked both the social position and the money to join a standard lodge and gratify their yearnings for distinction by wearing a plume and a sword. Many found the hood and robe a convenient shelter for daydreams and a promise of supernatural power by night. Klan ceremonies and parades fed the starving spirit of many non-conformist Protestants nursing a secret and undefined yearning for less scolding and more ritual in the church."[7]

The Klavern was often simply a single room equipped with an altar on which to lay an American flag, a Bible usually opened at Romans 12:1 as a guide to Christian life

("I beseech you therefore, brethren . . . that ye present your bodies a living sacrifice, holy, acceptable unto God, which is your reasonable service"), sometimes an unsheathed sword (representing determination to overcome obstacles to Christian living), and a container of initiation water for sprinkling on initiates to rid them of "alien defilement." The usual cross could not be set ablaze, but was illuminated by electric lights.

At first glance it may seem absurd that grown men could go through such rituals. Yet many other lodges and organizations then had—and still have—equally elaborate or occult ceremonies and regalia. The bizarre costumes of the Mystic Shriners or Knights of Pythias surely appealed to many, as did the Klan's robes and hoods. Masonic orders were also noted for secrecy. A popular illustration of the time, often found framed and hanging in the homes of Masons, showed a girl saying "I love to love a Mason 'cause a Mason never tells."

Americans were a nation of joiners, and, along with their various professed ideals and charitable works, each lodge had some ceremonies and regalia to appeal to the yearning for special status. The Klan, however, outdid all other lodges in mystical language and symbols. Colonel Simmons, helped by Clarke, had early adopted and greatly expanded the strange vocabulary of the old Reconstruction Klan to appeal to the prospective Klansman's love of mystery and need to feel special.

The Grand Dragon of the Realm was aided by nine "Hydras." The Great Titan of a Klan Province had his seven "Furies." An Exalted Cyclops of a local unit had his twelve "Terrors." There were also "Genii," "Goblins," and "Nighthawks" (couriers and investigators).

In one minor legal action filed by Stephenson in Indianapolis, the complaint in the Klan decree begins: "To all Genii, Grand Dragons, Hydras, Great Titans, Furies, Kleagles, Grand Goblins, Cyclops, Imperial Nighthawks, Terrors and Citizens of the Invisible Empire of the Realm of Indiana of the Knights of the Ku Klux Klan." For its mystical communications the Klan even had its own calendar, with May as the first month of the year and each day, week, and month having weird and fearful names. In this vein, Stephenson's complaint ends with: "Done on the Deadly Day of the Frightful Friday of the Weeping Week of the Bloody Month of the Fearful Year of the Knights of the Ku Klux Klan LVIII."[8] The Fearful Year LVIII in the Klan's mystical calendar was really 1924—the fifty-eighth year since the first Klan was formally organized in May 1866 in Pulaski, Tennessee, based on the small social club started there in December 1865. May, in the same calendar, became the first month of each year.

With some variations in calendar titles, similar language is found in a letter reportedly sent to Klansmen in 1924 by John L. Duvall, later elected mayor of Indianapolis with strong Klan support. The letter, revealed in several newspapers in 1926, was an appeal for Klansmen to work for the nomination of "our brother Klansman, Major [Ed] Jackson" for governor, and ends with: "Done by me, the great Klaliff of this province, in the wierd [sic] day of the woeful week, of the dreadful month, of the bloody moon, in the weeping year of the Klan—this 16th day of March." It was signed "J. L. Duvall." When it was revealed in 1926, Duvall charged it was a forgery. He denied having any official connection with the Klan and said he was never an officer.[9]

Private financial gain and moral fervor both played a role in swelling the Klan ranks. As Samuel Taylor Moore wrote in *The Independent* of December 13, 1924:

> A number of practical-minded Hoosiers saw in the Klan prosperous employment. Many joined as Kleagles to share in the harvest of klecktokens [initiation fees] or the $100.00-a-week salary of a Great Titan, or to enter some other titled and salaried position in the court of the Invisible Empire. . . . Many earnest farmers joined the Klan to use it as an instrument for moral crusading. The countryside felt postwar social unsettlement equally with the city dwellers. Bootleggers were thriving, moral standards were lowered. These farmers wished to remove temptation beyond their

sons and daughters. They directed their energies successfully to eliminate the liquor seller and the brothel keeper.

The cities were a different matter:

> While the Klan leaders hired private detectives to prose-
> cute city liquor sellers of foreign extraction, bootleggers who
> were eligible for Klan membership by reason of birth has-
> tened to join the Invisible Empire for protection. They found
> that which they sought, because the Klan oath of brother-
> hood (and secrecy) is inoperative only for the major crimes
> of murder, rape and treason. Thus, the Invisible Empire
> prospered both ways from the middle.[10]

Small businessmen often joined for what they perceived
to be an advantage over their rivals: the Klan would boycott
Catholic, Jewish, or foreign competitors. They often com-
pelled their employees to join the Klan so they could adver-
tise that they were "100 percent American." Other merchants who opposed the Klan at heart contributed their
ten-dollar membership fees to avoid harassment. "In the
final analysis," Moore wrote, "it was blackmail."

Workers in some factories with a Klan foreman soon
found that membership in the Klan was the key to promotion or even keeping a job. Frank Chandler, an Evansville
librarian, recalled his own father's experience as a worker
in a furniture factory. "One day," says Chandler, "my father
was told he'd better join [the Klan] or else find another job.
So what did he do? He joined." The Klan sometimes saw
labor organizers as "Bolsheviks," and its antiunion stand
could lead some factory owners to look the other way; the
more Klan members in the factory, the less labor trouble.
However, it didn't always work that way. The superinten-
dent of employment for the street railway in Indianapolis,
for example, was fired after twenty years' service when his
superiors found he would hire only Klan members to operate the streetcars. He was apparently not union busting,
but only acting out of his own religious intolerance.[11]

Klan favoritism ran through police departments, sheriff's offices, and courthouse staffs. Reporters known to be

anti-Klan often found access to police information or court records more difficult. Many people did, indeed, oppose the Klan, seeing it as a socially disruptive force, but few spoke out. In communities where the Klan became a power, there was always a strong undercurrent of anti-Klan sentiment, but this feeling was usually expressed with caution. Reporters often found Klan opponents not wishing to be quoted.

As in many other states, the Klan in Indiana relied heavily on support from members of the Masonic lodges. Masonic leaders often denounced the Klan as a divisive force. But the Masons had a traditional anti-Romanist bias. When Klan Kleagles set out to organize a community, they often sought out first the aid of influential Masons. Readers of the Klan's *Fiery Cross* often found it filled with Masonic news. They were repeatedly urged to subscribe also to the *Fellowship Forum*, a Masonic publication, with application blanks printed for their convenience.

As Marion Monteval wrote of the Klan in general (not only in Indiana):

> Propagation of the Klan was directed from the beginning to a conquest of the Masonic fraternity. Nearly all of the organizers sent into the field and commissioned as Kleagles were members of the Masonic fraternity. These men wore Masonic emblems and symbols as passports to the leaders in Masonry in every community. . . . Some of them wore as many as three Masonic emblems conspicuously displayed. . . . These Kleagles were instructed in founding the Klan in a new community to first of all enlist Masons in good standing, and through them find ready access to the lodges and around them as a nucleus to organize a Klan.[12]

It was no coincidence that Hiram Evans, a Texas Klan Great Titan, became Imperial Kligrapp (national secretary) in the Klan's Imperial Kloncilium after he had quelled a dispute with Texas Masons. The Masonic incident was one thing that had attracted the attention of then-Imperial Wizard, Simmons. (Little did Simmons suspect that Evans would soon be taking over his job as top man of the Klan headquarters.)

Opposition by the press seems to have had results opposite of what was intended. The editor of the Klan's major newspaper in the South, the *Imperial Knight Hawk*, was close to the mark when he wrote: "The press of the country has, more than any one agency, increased the membership of the Knights of the Ku Klux Klan to what it is today. From the press the Klan has received gratis and is still receiving daily, advertisement [sic] that is worth millions in cold cash. . . . Never have the newspapers seeking to do men or a movement an evil turn so completely, and to their own astonishment, done a good one."[13]

In Indiana, when the Klan first appeared, many newspapers openly opposed it. The *New York World*'s exposés of Klan atrocities elsewhere were still fresh in the public mind. Then, as the Invisible Empire mushroomed as a popular champion of God, flag, and country, many papers withdrew into a neutral position. On April 24, 1922, for example, the *Indianapolis News* editorialized that "the odium of the [Klan] name" persisted. "The tactical methods of the reformed Klansmen have not cleared it of its offensiveness. It got off to a bad start and has not improved its position. Nor will it as long as most citizens refuse to be either frightened or misled by adult boys in grotesque masks who seek to exploit a primitive fear of ghosts." Soon, however, as Indiana Klansmen and their supporters grew into the hundreds of thousands, the *News* confined itself largely to routine reporting of occasional Klan public appearances. Such editorial denunciations moderated or disappeared.

A major exception was the *Indianapolis Times*. As the Klan grew, the *Times*, braving inevitable circulation losses, made an editorial decision to fight it. By the 1924 general election, it would be carrying condemnations of the Klan and its candidate for governor, Ed Jackson, on its front pages (see Chapter 6, pages 118–119). Other, smaller papers, that opposed the Klan in one way or another, included the *Ft. Wayne Journal-Gazette* which had a large Catholic circulation, the *South Bend Tribune* (in the home area of

Catholic Notre Dame University), the *Richmond Palladium*, the *Vincennes Commercial*, and, of course, several black weeklies in Indianapolis. They were, however, at least among the white-owned publications, a minority. Most, like the *Indianapolis News*, as well as the *Indianapolis Star*, seemed to prefer the safer neutral ground.

The few opponents of the Klan who took direct action at the street level almost always did it anonymously. Sometimes bushels of carpet tacks were found in the path of Klan paraders. Nobody except the perpetrators knew who did it, and the Klan press dismissed them as un-American hoodlums.

Sometimes Klan parades were interrupted by carefully placed false fire alarms. At least three such alarms were set off during a huge Klan parade in downtown Indianapolis on the night of May 24, following the Klan political victories at the 1924 Indiana State Republican convention.[14] On the same night one Klansman returning from the parade carrying his hood and robe under his arm was attacked by three teenage boys who took away his regalia and ran with it. The *Indianapolis News*, reporting the incident on May 26, 1924, identified the attackers as "Italian boys."

Early on the morning of July 4, 1923, Klansmen passing through Indianapolis on their way to the tristate rally in Kokomo were threatened by a crowd at the interurban railway terminal station, and later their car was stoned. The Klan interurban car arrived at the Indianapolis station shortly after midnight. Several of the Klansmen had gone into the lunchroom when a crowd of young men gathered outside, hissing and booing and challenging them to come out. The Klansmen didn't respond, but a waiter called the police after he was later assaulted by mistake. The Klan car continued on its way, but as it proceeded north on Capitol Avenue at Wabash Street, an unidentified assailant threw a rock through the car's window.[15]

As a "100 percent American" organization, the Klan attracted many war veterans, but not all. American Legion posts were often divided on the Klan issue, and some veterans openly opposed the Klan. One was Hiram Bearss of Peru, Indiana, a hero of the Spanish-American War and a marine veteran of World War I, known as "Hiking Hiram" due to a limp from war injuries. As a candidate for Congress in 1922, he denounced the Klan and lost the election.

A few weeks later, on Saturday afternoon, December 16, 1922, after an initiation ceremony in a nearby woods, the Klan was parading down Peru's main street. Hiram, still smarting from his defeat, got into his car and drove directly into the parade. Klansmen surrounded his car, opened the door, and pummeled Bearss as he sat at the wheel. Then they demanded that he salute the flag that they were carrying. Hiram grabbed a wrench, got out of the car, and shouted: "Salute the flag? You goddamn sons of bitches. I salute the flag when it's properly carried. I've followed the flag where you Kluxers would be afraid to look at on a map. Come on, you Kluxers, one and all. I'll take on the lot of you!" Other people came to Hiram's aid, and the Klansmen left without further disturbance.[16]

Another Klan clash with veterans came in 1924, when the Rainbow Division Veterans Association invited a Catholic priest, Father Patrick Duffy, chaplain of the "Fighting 69th" regiment, to speak at its national convention in Indianapolis. The Klan said the Catholic priest's presence would be "unpatriotic and un-American" and sent a committee of Klan veterans to protest. One of the Rainbow veterans told them, "You go to hell! Father Duffy was in the Rainbow and this division knew no question of creed. He is one of our buddies and he is going to speak and if you people don't like it you can get the hell off the stage."[17]

While the Klan found active support among many Protestant pastors, some openly and courageously rejected it. One such profile in courage was the Reverend Clay Trusty, pastor of the Seventh Christian Church in Indianapolis. His church was located on the city's near northwest side (near 30th Street and Northwestern Avenue). The area contained a mixture of whites, blacks, Protestants, and Catholics.

One of his sons, Clay Trusty, Jr., former assistant managing editor of the *Indianapolis News*, was only six years old when the Klan issue arose, but from his own and family memories he recalls the events that finally forced the Reverend Trusty out of his job. "The members of my Dad's church were Klansmen almost to the man," he said. "Mother told me many times how Dad would preach against the Klan Sunday after Sunday, knowing he was digging his own grave."

Even before the Klan blossomed, the Reverend Trusty had taken leadership in establishing a community center, through donations from businesses and individuals. He decided to organize a church basketball league, made up of all churches in the area, including Holy Angels Catholic Church. "His board of directors threw a fit over that," Clay, Jr., recalled. "They informed him there would be no Catholics playing ball in the 'Comm House' as it was called. Dad told them he had raised the money for the center and that if the Catholics weren't allowed to play in the gym he would board it up. This was the end for Dad. He was 'asked to resign' his pastorate, but it was outright firing."

One man who stood by him was a man named Davidson, whom Clay, Jr., remembers only as "Davie." "Dad and Davie were in charge of the education committee of the ministerial association. This committee was responsible for, among other things, the religion classes held weekly at the YMCA. In sheer defiance of the association membership, they invited as speakers for the classes within a few weeks of each other Bishop Chartrand of the Catholic church and Rabbi Feuerlicht of the Hebrew Congregation." Both managed to speak but "this, needless to say, nearly blew the lid off the association."

On another occasion, Clay, Jr., remembers, his father came home with a new four-door Willys-Knight automobile and "surprised the family."

At dinner that night he announced we would all take a ride up north near Golden Hill to see a little party that was going to be held. We all piled into the car and drove to 37th and Clifton Streets where there was a big vacant lot near the plush Golden Hill-Woodstock area. It was dark but a bonfire had been started and there was a crowd of men in white gowns and hoods milling about. I don't recall the speaking but I'm sure there was some. Then they set fire to a cross and Dad told us, "That's for me." Many of them were obviously members of his own congregation. . . ." Dad resigned his pastorate and we changed our membership to Central Christian Church, along with the Stalnaker family [Cecil Stalnaker, who was also among the few who stood with the Reverend Trusty in his fight against the Klan]. His health began failing shortly afterward, but he did some fill-in preaching in small towns. . . . About two years after his forced resignation, Dad died.[18]

The Reverend Trusty was succeeded briefly at the Seventh Christian Church by the Reverend Gerald L. K. Smith, a notorious rabble-rousing bigot and anti-Semite.

Meanwhile, despite all opposition, the Klan only grew stronger. Beneath it all lay the Puritan spirit so well described by Robert Coughlan:

> The Puritan morality that inspired *The Scarlet Letter* and the hanging of witches spread across the country not far behind the moving frontier . . . but Puritanism defies human nature, and human nature repressed emerges in disguise. The fleshly appetites of the small townsmen when confronted by the rigid moral standards of his social environment may be transformed into a fanatic persecution of those very appetites. The Klan, which sanctified chastity and "clean living" and brought punishment to sinners was a perfect outlet for those repressions.[19]

No "sinners" were lynched in Indiana. There is no record of floggings or tar-and-feather parties, as in some other states. But the Klansmen found an outlet in raids on bootleggers, gambling dives, and brothels, especially through the resurrection of a nineteenth-century establishment originally called the Horse Thief Protection Association, later the Horse Thief Detective Association.

In 1865, in the backwash from the Civil War, the old National Trails through central Indiana had become thoroughfares for many rootless, disreputable characters. Horse thievery was rampant. In response, the state legislature of that year enacted the Horse Thief Act (Laws of Indiana, 1863–69, Chap. XCV, page 196). The law authorized the organization of volunteer constabularies in which, as it stated, "any number of persons, citizens of the State of Indiana, not less than ten, may and they are hereby authorized to form themselves into a company for the purpose of detecting and apprehending horse thieves and other felons and for mutual protection and indemnity against the act of such horse thieves and felons."

Once membership rolls were submitted to local authorities and the companies duly authorized, the members were "in pursuit and arrest of horse thieves and other offenders against the criminal laws of the state" to have "all the power of constables."

As time went on, both the horse thieves and the constabularies virtually disappeared. But in the 1920s, the Horse Thief Act was still on the books and it was made to order for the Ku Klux Klan. Among his other strokes of opportunism, Stephenson resurrected the Horse Thief Act as authority for a special Klan enforcement arm, which grew rapidly. By spring 1924, at least twenty-five thousand were regularly qualified constables of what was now called the Horse Thief Detective Association. Of this total, an estimated twenty-two thousand were Klansmen. They were authorized to carry weapons, make arrests, and, "in the absence of warrants, to hold [arrested persons] in custody without warrant." (Strict application of the Constitution to the states was still far away.)

The companies had to be authorized by county commissioners. In the 1920s, with growing demands for law and order, this was easily secured. The Horse Thief Detectives raided bootleggers and gambling dives, sometimes with,

sometimes without the cooperation of regular peace officers. In one series of sensational raids in Indianapolis, 125
persons were arrested on charges of operating speakeasies
or gambling dives and buying liquor, with wholesale convictions following.

In other communities the Klan also made itself a law
enforcement power. Klan leaders claimed that from June
1922 to October 1923, more than three-thousand cases of
prohibition law violations were brought to Indiana courts,
largely through the efforts of the Klan's Horse Thief Detectives.[20]

Sometimes there were excesses, such as Klan agents
stopping and searching automobiles, a practice that finally
drew protests from national automobile clubs. But the
Horse Thief Detectives had strong popular support, even
among non-Klansmen. They were seen as simply helping
to enforce the law, a far cry from the illegal terrorist
violence associated with the Klan of the South and Southwest.

At best, however, they were a nuisance and sometimes an
unduly intimidating force, especially to young couples on
lovers' lanes. William E. Wilson, son of an anti-Klan congressman who was defeated in his bid for re-election in
1924, describes his own experience with the horse thief
detectives in Evansville in the summer of that year.

> I found a new girl that summer and for a while we
> thought we were in love, but I never learned where she or
> her family stood on the Klan. She would not talk about it.
> Almost every time I took her out, my car was trailed by the
> Horse Thief Detective Association, which was the police
> force of the Klan. It was always the same car that did the
> trailing, and I finally got used to it. It would pick me up
> about a block from our house and follow me to the girl's
> house, and wait while I went in to get her, and then follow
> us to the movies or wherever we were going. When we came
> out, it was there waiting and would follow us home. One
> night, when I eluded its shadow and parked on a country
> road with her, a farmer pulled up beside us and said, "If you
> kids know what's good for you, you'll move along. The

Kluxers are patrolling this road tonight, and God knows what they'll do to you if they catch you here. . . . I took my girl home.[21]

The Horse Thief Detectives were not the only ones whose zealotry led to extremes. The Klan passion to "clean up" communities at almost any cost sometimes reached into the courts as well. A classic case was that of Clarence W. Dearth, in 1922 elected judge of Delaware County Circuit Court in Muncie with strong Klan backing. Dearth taught Muncie's largest adult Bible class, in the leading Methodist church. He was an ardent crusader against bootlegging, gambling, and prostitution. He was also a member of the Ku Klux Klan.

As Clell Maple, a prominent manufacturer and one-time friend of Dearth, later described him: "Judge Dearth was a member of the Ku Klux Klan when I was. I admired him greatly because of the high-minded talks he made to our organization." During a visit to the judge's home, Maple said, Dearth told him of his "personal expedition" into Muncie's "red-light district" and how he had paid for the services of two Indianapolis detectives out of his own pocket to check up on the brothels.

"Dearth told me he was tired of conditions and, raising his voice, said: 'Do you think I am going to stand for conditions like that? If John Hampton [the mayor] does not clean up this town I'll try him and impeach him. . . . I personally have seen gambling in cigar stores in Muncie, and as the father of two growing boys want to see it stopped.'"[22]

To get his way, Judge Dearth needed to make sure juries in criminal trials went along with him, even on questionable or illegally seized evidence. As later charged, he manipulated jury selections so that he might personally control them. Among other things, he appointed a puppet, Jake Cavanaugh, as jury commissioner to do his bidding in getting favorable jury panels. Cavanaugh was not a property "freeholder" as required by law for the job. As a cover,

Dearth deeded him a small twenty-by-twenty-foot plot, worth about twenty-five dollars, to keep him in his position.

It was also later charged that Dearth had aided in and sanctioned "irregular drawing of juries, prepared lists of jurors from a telephone directory, approved calls for persons for jury duty who had served on juries within a year," contrary to law, and the illegal placing of at least twenty-five persons on jury panels within a period of a few months in early 1927.[23] However, what finally sparked action against him was his fight with George Dale, the fifty-five-year-old editor of the Muncie weekly newspaper, the *Post-Democrat*. Against fearsome odds, Dale had long opposed the Klan, in exposés and editorials.

Muncie was a Klan hotbed. Dale had been waylaid and pummeled. Women of the Klan auxiliaries had spat upon him in the streets. His life had been threatened. Dale repeatedly attacked Dearth in his paper, charging that juries had been fixed and that the criminal laws were not being equitably enforced. Dearth ordered the paper suppressed. When Dale defied him, Dearth charged him with contempt of court and ordered him to pay a five-hundred-dollar fine and serve six months in jail. The case was appealed four times. Ultimately, after the U.S. Supreme Court refused to hear it, Dale was pardoned by Governor Jackson, who was by then apparently seeking to distance himself from his own former Klan connections.

Meanwhile, Muncie sentiment had begun to swing against Dearth and toward Dale. The Klan was dwindling in the wake of the Stephenson scandal. The incident that finally brought things to a head was Dearth's treatment of newsboys selling the *Post-Democrat*. An anonymous letter had appeared in the paper, charging Dearth with judicial misconduct. The letter later turned out to be from Clell Maple, who also had decided Dearth had gone too far.

Dearth had police round up at least thirty-five newsboys selling the issue of the paper and bring them into his court. Their newspapers were taken away, and they were warned not to sell any more under threat of legal action. Outraged

Muncie citizens soon began calling for Dearth's impeachment. One leader in organizing petitions for impeachment
was F. L. Bodkin, president of the Municipal League of
Muncie. Soon petitions containing hundreds of signatures
were presented to the state legislature.

In a front-page editorial supporting the impeachment,
the *Indianapolis Times* said:

> Neither *The Times* or the people of the state are specially
> interested in whether vice, gambling and bootlegging flour-
> ish in Muncie. They are not particularly interested in
> whether it is protected or not. That is a matter for the
> citizens of Muncie. [But] suppression of the press does inter-
> est every citizen, not only in Indiana but of the nation.
>
> Judge Dearth has outraged the Constitution of the State
> of Indiana and the Constitution of the United States. . . . He
> established himself as the sole judge of what shall be printed
> in newspapers and asserted that power in a manner more
> tyrannical than ever before has been exerted or attempted
> in the history of any state.
>
> Other judges have stretched their power to punish for
> contempt until public conscience rebelled. This judge has
> done more. He has forcibly and physically suppressed an
> issue of a newspaper because it contained an article criticiz-
> ing himself. . . . Shall the word go out that free speech and a
> free press no longer exist in Indiana?[24]

Articles of impeachment against Dearth were filed in the
state legislature on March 4, 1927. He was indicted on
seven charges, including jury manipulation and suppression of the press. His trial in the state senate began later
the same month. One dramatic moment in the trial came
when John Raines, a fourteen-year-old newsboy, told the
senators how he had been arrested for selling copies of the
Post-Democrat after Dearth's suppression order. He said a
police officer arrested him and took him into the courthouse
to face the judge, who immediately confiscated all of his
papers. The boy was asked:

"Was any writ or paper of any kind read to you?"

"No," the boy said.

"Did the judge say anything?"

"He told me to get out and if I sold any more papers he would put me on probation."

"What did you do then?"

"I went out and got some more papers and sold them until another policeman chased me up an alley and put his hand on his revolver and told me to stop. He took me to the courthouse and smacked me. The judge said nothing more but sent for my father." At this point, the testimony was interrupted by an outburst of applause for the newsboy. The lieutenant-governor, presiding at the senate hearing, rapped for order.

A majority of the senate voted for Dearth's conviction on five of seven impeachment counts charging various acts of judicial misconduct. But a two-thirds vote was needed, and the majority fell two votes short. Dearth returned to the Muncie bench. Nevertheless, it was the first time in ninety-two years that an Indiana official had faced impeachment charges in the state senate, and at the root of it lay the insidious zealotry of the Ku Klux Klan.

Dale's fight with the Klan had attracted national attention. As praise for Dale's courage came in from out of town, Muncie's attitude began to change even further. By 1930, Dale would be elected Muncie's mayor.

5

The Military Machine

AS THE MAJOR ELECTION YEAR of 1924 approached, the Indiana Realm of the Ku Klux Klan was nearing its zenith of political power. As many as 300,000 members were ready to do its bidding and a finely tuned intelligence network reached into every precinct of the state.

"Here at last," wrote Samuel Tait, Jr., "was a political weapon calculated to satisfy all the fear and hatreds the evangelical hell-hounds had been instilling in the faithful for so long; fear of the power of Rome; hatred of the wickedness of the cities; fear of the Darwinism heresy, and hatred of the individualist who persisted in having a private stock [of liquor]."[1]

It was formidable, but it was still a sort of shadow world. It was not a political party in any usual sense. It had no voter registration rolls. It published no open political advertising in major newspapers. Nobody campaigned in a hood and robe. For many politicians, the Klan posed a dilemma. To openly oppose it would surely risk defeat. To openly support it would risk losing the still sizeable anti-Klan vote. In either case, in any close contest, the balance could go either way.

Those who courted Klan support sometimes simply made

speeches they hoped would find Klan favor down the line—speeches lauding Americanism, separation of church and state, enforcement of prohibition laws, hopefully in terms general enough not to alienate any large segment of anti-Klan voters. Others made deals behind the scenes. In 1927, preparing evidence for a trial to revoke the Klan's state corporate charter, Indiana's attorney-general Arthur Gilliom took depositions from many present and former Klansmen. The Klan was by then in disarray, and many were ready to talk. Gilliom's term ended before the trial could take place, but his records were made available to the Indiana State Library and the State Archives of Indiana.

Stephenson, then in prison but anxious for revenge on those he felt had betrayed him, talked freely to Gilliom about the contracts the Klan got from political candidates.

"The practice," Stephenson said, "was to take contracts from [the candidates] in which they agree, in case of their election, to appoint only those approved by the Klan. In the case of Congressmen, through the Great Titan of the Congressional district; in the case of the Governor, through the Grand Dragon; in the case of the mayor of a city, through the leader of that unit that covered his city."[2] Sometimes these contracts were verbal and general, sometimes written and specific. One such specific agreement—a written pledge to Stephenson from Duvall in early 1925, when he was campaigning, successfully, for mayor of Indianapolis—was revealed during a 1926 Marion County grand jury investigation. It said: "In return for the support of D. C. Stephenson, in the event that I am elected Mayor of Indianapolis, Indiana, I promise not to appoint any person as a member of the board of public works without they [sic] first have the endorsement of D. C. Stephenson. I fully agree and promise to appoint Claude Worley as Chief of Police and Earl Klinck [one of Stephenson's bodyguards] a Captain."[3] Headquartered in Indianapolis, Stephenson was apparently considered leader of the Klan unit covered Duvall's city.

Candidates in Indiana and elsewhere were often asked to promise that they would not appoint any Roman Catholics.

(Harry Truman, running for a county judgeship in Independence, Missouri, in 1922 said he was asked to make such a promise in return for Klan support—a deal he said he angrily rejected.)[4]

Stephenson's interest in the Indianapolis Board of Public Works, with its control over lucrative city contracts, was undoubtedly rooted in his interest in money as well as power. In the same early spring 1925, through his allies in the state legislature, he tried but failed to reshape the state roads commission to his personal advantage. He had, however, earlier received undercover promises from Governor Jackson to make appointments that would give him control of the state purchasing agency in return for his support in the 1924 elections. It could be a gold mine for Stephenson's coal business. Influence with the police was also important. Worley did, in fact, become chief of the Indianapolis police department, though by that time Stephenson was on trial for murder.

Politicians hoped that the secrecy of the Klan itself would enable them to avoid it as an issue altogether, or at least give them a neutral image. A political correspondent for the *Baltimore Sun* told of an after-hours poker game in a middle western newspaper office, where one player was a genial congressman who got along well with the working press:

> Someone tried to tease him by making up a story about a new Congressional resolution for an investigation of the Klan. The politician suddenly became unhappily serious. "That is nothing to joke about!" he said, "Not even in whispers. That stuff runs like quicksilver. There are thousands of those fellows [Klansmen] in my district. But I don't know they are there. Nobody will be able to prove that they are there. If I don't know they are in my district I am not called upon to express an opinion about them, that's what I'm doing. That's the only thing to do."[5]

However, simply avoiding the Klan in Indiana wasn't easy. A major reason was the detailed political apparatus that Stephenson called his Military Machine (no doubt from memories of the army structure he had left only a few years earlier.) It was a near-perfect model for any ideological or evangelical political pressure group that could command the votes of its followers down the line.

First, each of Indiana's ninety-two counties was organized into a Klanton, headed by an Exalted Cyclops—a post similar to that of a county political party chairman. Each Congressional district became a Klan Province, directed by a Great Titan, who in political terms commanded a following similar to that of a district party chairman, or even a congressman. Klan officials were elected by the members in their jurisdictions. The state was a Realm, under Grand Dragon—D. C. Stephenson, whose orders usually went down the line under the title of "G-1." In the military residuum of Stephenson's mind, the county Klan boss was a colonel, the district chief was a brigadier-general, and he himself the commanding general of all.

Stephenson often used the title "G-1" for specific orders, "The Old Man" for more general statements of policy. In the army, the "G-1" was, and is, a general staff officer in charge of personnel. Whether Stephenson meant this, or simply thought it would sound impressive, is uncertain.

At the lower levels, a major and his staff were in command of wards or towns, with a captain for each ward, lieutenants commanding precincts, and under them an array of sergeants and corporals to keep direct touch with the rank-and-file. The titles could sometimes become confusing, as when George Coffin, Stephenson's choice for chairman of the Marion County Republican organization, was referred to as Captain Coffin. Norman Weaver said:

> The Military Machine was the ward organization of the Klan. The ward-heelers and door-bell ringers of the Klan were the [rank-and-file] members of the Military Machine. These were the men who did the active political work of the Klan at the local levels. Klan leaders would have schemed and boasted in vain but for the members of the Military Machine who made certain voters got to the polls and voted

correctly. Without them the political program of the Indiana Klan would have ended in failure.[6]

Still, an air of mystery surrounded the whole apparatus. Most voters knew who their regular county political party chairman was. But for most outside the Klan, the Exalted Cyclops remained a sort of shadow they had heard about but didn't fully comprehend.

Stephenson told Gilliom he had put plans for his Military Machine into force in "every county of the state of Indiana and in several other states." However, there is little evidence that this machine worked in other states with half the efficiency that it did in Indiana. There, Stephenson called for a list of all names, addresses, phone numbers, occupations, employers, and other detailed data on every officer in the machine. He wanted an organization he could direct and control simply by picking up one of several telephones on his desk in Indianapolis.

Samuel Bemenderfer, an associate of Stephenson, told about a conversation he had with him in 1923, when the Grand Dragon was perfecting his machine:

> He said there was to be established a telephone system which would go directly from his office to the headquarters of the different officers in each county, which controlled the military organization and the instructions would go direct from his office over this private wire to every county in the state, and in turn from the military directory in each county, they would go direct to the other officers, and it would pyramid—each man would be responsible to get that message to his officers."[7]

A striking example of the thoroughness with which Stephenson kept track of the political scene and climate is shown in his *Field Regulations No. 3*, which he issued to his officers down the line on May 6, 1923, in the name of "G1—N" (N for national). The instructions began innocently enough.

> Each organization will forthwith:
> 1. Establish each week a program in which one outstand-

ing thing for the betterment of the community will be accomplished. (Such service may be rendered by aiding the public schools, ministerial associations, or any benevolent organization, or any civic body. . . .)

2. Make a written report each week to State Headquarters, outlining the activities and accomplishments for the preceding week.

Such activities to polish the Klan's public image were standard operating procedure and, of course, a valuable spur to new membership. But then the instructions begin to assume a Gestapo character:

3. Procure the name, address, and vocation of every individual of voting age, in each county, township, and precinct, falling within the following classifications:
   (a) All Aliens or Foreigners.
   (b) I.W.W.'s [Industrial Workers of the World], Bolshevists [sic], Reds, or Agitators.
   (c) Every bootlegger, or other individuals engaged in any way in the manufacture, sale, or distribution of liquor.
   (d) All owners, operators, or inmates of houses of prostitution.
   (e) All Jews.
   (f) All Negroes.
   (g) All Roman Catholics.

4. Secure accurate reports and evidence of meetings of any association, group, gathering or organization of whatsoever nature interested in or connected with the propagation, development or protection of the interest of any group, or groups classified under paragraph 3 of these instructions. Wherever such evidence is secured, make a written report to the state office covering the nature, location, hour of meeting and what transpired.

5. Secure and transmit to State Headquarters the name, address, rank of office, nationality, place of birth, age, political and religious affiliations of the following individuals:
   (a) County Officials.
   (b) State Officials.

   (c) District Court Officials.
   (d) School Boards.
   (e) School Faculties.
   (f) Truant Officers.
   (g) Police Force.
   (h) Library Board.
   (i) Fire Department and so forth.

Do not fail to state the *religious affiliation of the wife and the school affiliations of the children* [italics added] of each of the above classified officers, as well as the attitude of each toward this organization. (If antagonistic to our organization, state clearly the character of his attack upon us, and what you are doing to combat it.)

6. You will secure and transmit to State Headquarters the name and address of every newspaper published within the bounds of your territorial jurisdiction together with:

   (a) Its political policy.
   (b) Name and address of controlling stockholders, or owners.
   (c) Name, address, nationality, and religious affiliation of the editors whether "for" "neutral" or "against" us and whether editor is a member of our organization.

Following these come instructions to make reports on "law violators arrested within your territorial jurisdiction," and wherever arrests are made to "give the nationality" and "religious faith" of the arrested person; also that "no county organization will permit any individual within its jurisdiction to speak in public as its authorized representative, unless such speaker has been properly O.K.'d by State Headquarters."

At the conclusion of *Field Regulations No. 3* comes the following exhortation:

Bear in mind constantly that single-handed enthusiasm, inspired by justice and spurred on by the conviction of eternal right will move mountainous barriers where an army of ordinary workers would not create a tremor of interest. It was the enthusiastic sincerity of Napoleon [whose bust adorned Stephenson's desk in his Indianapolis office] that conquered Europe, and it was the burning torch of enthusiastic devotion which emblazoned in letters of fire the teachings of the Master; and it will be the enthusiasm which will keep aglow the torch of patriotic devotion so deep-set in the Spirit of the Klan.[8]

"D. C. Stephenson was convinced that the Klan could give him control of Indiana," Weaver wrote, and "the military machine was his means for seizing control."[9] But he also realized that to win elections he must have support beyond the Klan itself. In one memorandum to his officers down the line, on October 24, 1924, he said: "You must realize that we cannot win this fight [the November elections] with the Klan vote alone. We must secure all Protestant support."[10]

Once a slate of candidates was decided upon and printed, it was widely distributed. Sometimes the sheets were rolled and fixed with clothespins and tossed on front porches at the dawn of election day. Near the polling places, Klansmen, with no regalia to identify them, passed out the sheets to people on their way to vote. Just before the 1924 primary elections in South Bend, Indiana, the Klan got copies of all Protestant Sunday school papers and spent all of one Saturday night slipping the ballot of Klan favorites into each paper, expecting, of course, that they would be passed on to the children's parents. In many communities, ladies of the Klan auxiliaries provided baby-sitting services for women voters.

Often voters were uncertain or confused as to who was doing all of this. Klansmen near the polling places wore no hoods or robes. The ballots of Klan-favored candidates bore no garish Klan inscriptions. If any exhortations were included, they were most often simply appeals to "100 percent Americanism" or "Christian values."

Black voters, largely concentrated in Indianapolis, seem to have been more aware of Klan pressures than others. Most Klan favorites were Republicans, but a byword among many blacks was "Abe Lincoln ain't running this year." On one primary election day, members of the Klan's Horse Thief Detective Association paraded through Indianapolis's black neighborhoods waving their pistols in the air.

Still, the Klan machine remained a shadowy if powerful force for most voters. As Weaver wrote, Stephenson's machine "served its purpose of transferring power from legitimate channels to special channels created by a secret organization . . . and was a model that might at any time be copied by any other pressure group that wishes to transform itself into a political force."[11]

It was with this powerful political apparatus that Stephenson set out in 1924 to consolidate his hold on Indiana and, looking toward 1928, secure a possible Republican nomination for president. He was a power to be reckoned with, but by now he was no longer the undisputed boss of the Klan in Indiana. Down in Atlanta, at national Klan headquarters, Imperial Wizard Evans had begun to have misgivings about the man he had made a Grand Dragon.

First, Stephenson had become a bigger power in the Klan's northern wing than Evans expected. His following went far beyond Indiana; he had national political ambitions; he was a threat to the throne. "The fight for control of the Klan between Stephenson and Evans was bound to come," said Irving Leibowitz. "Both were bent on absolute power and both were utterly ruthless and unscrupulous."[12]

Second, insiders' stories of Stephenson's drunkenness and lechery had reached Atlanta: his attempted drunken rape of a manicurist in a Columbus, Ohio, hotel room; the orgies in his Irvington mansion; his attempted seductions of several women, in states from Georgia to Indiana. None of these things had come to light in any court of law. Stephenson was apparently able to keep them hushed up with his money or influence. But by fall 1923, Evans and his agents were in Indiana gathering evidence for the Klan's own use, and Stephenson knew it.

In a telegram to "Dr. H. W. Evans, Room 1528, Washington Hotel, Indianapolis, Indiana," Stephenson, then in Columbus, said in part:

> I have been very much grieved to learn that you were in Indianapolis, engaged in a campaign to assassinate my character, and to know that this was your process of disposing of anyone who stood in the way of your cohorts. . . . If you insist on going further with your attack upon my personal integrity I shall be compelled to write a page in the history of these days which will be the final answer to the vulgar cowardly lies which are now being directed at me and which all honorable men will resent with a decision which will rock the foul cesspools of hate and jealousy which now flood the dollar-grabbers in Atlanta. . . . I challenge you or any of your cohorts to meet me before any organization in the state of Indiana and sustain the foul lies which Comer and Christy [two of Evans's agents] and others have circulated in Indianapolis during the past twenty-four hours.[13]

One powerful weapon in Stephenson's arsenal was the *Fiery Cross*, the major Klan weekly newspaper in Indiana as well as its neighboring realms. Estimates of its circulation in 1923 ranged up to a half-million. The *Fiery Cross*, first called *Facts*, had been started in Indianapolis by Ernest Reichard, Max Hartley, and William Boyer. Later it came under the editorship of Milton Elrod. Stephenson gained editorial control of the paper in early 1923. By late 1923 he was using it in a steady drumfire of attacks against Evans and the "Southern crowd" of the Klan. In articles signed simply "The Old Man" he denounced them as "ignoramuses," "rebels and deviations from Klan ideals," along with misappropriation of Klan money.

Later Evans regained control. Elrod resigned as editor and went to Washington, D.C., as head of a Klan bureau of education and publication, with an office in Evans's suite in the Capital. Stephenson nevertheless continued his attacks on Evans and his faction through speeches and telegrams, calling them "Southern dogs" and "damn rebels."

In another document to the "faithful sons of Hoosierdom" and entitled "The Old Man's Answer to Hate Venders," [sic]

Stephenson attacked Evans and the Atlanta Klan wing
even more directly, bringing in references to the Civil War:
"The hour of fate has struck. The venality and jealousy of
the men who carried the rebel flag in '61 is now invading
Indiana." It was, he said "a cowardly attempt on the part of
a few "yellow-livered" Southerners who hate everything
that is pure through the State of Indiana."

Of Evans himself, Stephenson said:

> The present national head [of the Klan] is an ignorant,
> uneducated, uncouth individual who eats his peas with his
> knife. He has neither courage nor culture. He cannot talk
> intelligently and he cannot keep a coherent conversation
> going on any subject for five minutes. His speeches are
> written by hired intelligence. The only thing he has ever
> been known to do was launch an attack upon the character
> and integrity of men eminent in talent and virtue.[14]

By now there were actually two Klan Grand Dragons in
Indiana. In January 1924, Stephenson had been put on trial
by the Evansville Klan chapter for "gross dereliction,"
including charges that he had tried to seduce a young
Evansville woman and had committed "numerous other
immoralities in Columbus, Ohio; Columbus, Indiana; in
Atlanta, Georgia; and on boats and trains." He was secretly
found guilty and "banished."

Within a few months Stephenson resigned as Grand
Dragon, then called an Indianapolis rump convention of
Klan representatives from around the state and had himself elected Grand Dragon of an autonomous Indiana Klan,
independent of Atlanta. In late 1924, he told a reporter that
he had no connection with the Klan since his resignation,
and that the Klan had become "anathema" to him. Yet
Samuel Taylor Moore quotes a Klan message of May 12,
1924, as follows:

> The assembled Klansmen of Indiana today, with 91 of 92
> counties represented, after full deliberation, decided to take
> control of their own organization. This does not mean seces-
> sion from the national organization, but means that the

strongest and most effective Klan state in the nation will henceforth formulate its own policies and elect its own officers, both local and state, and keep local funds in their local treasury . . . The assembly today elected D. C. Stephenson Grand Dragon, with a full quota of State officers from every part of the state.[15]

For his own Indiana Grand Dragon, Evans chose Walter F. Bossert, of Liberty, Indiana, who was then a Grand Klaliff (vice-president) of the Indiana Realm. Bossert took over the part of the Indiana Klan remaining loyal to Evans. It was sizable, but Stephenson continued as the dominant power in Indiana.

Meanwhile Stephenson saw another conspiracy—possibly an assassination effort—in the explosions and fire that destroyed his luxurious yacht, the *Reomar II*, at its mooring place in the lagoon of the Toledo (Ohio) Yacht Club shortly after 3:00 A.M. on June 27, 1924. He said "unscrupulous" enemies in the Klan had hoped to find him aboard, which he was not. He hired private detectives to conduct his own investigation. He also filed suit against Evans and Bossert in the federal court in Indianapolis, charging them with conspiring to destroy his vessel and asking damages of fifteen thousand dollars. The suit was later dismissed for lack of jurisdiction.

Then, on December 15 of the same year, investigators for the Ohio State Fire Marshal's Office announced that John H. Brady, age forty-nine, of Muncie, Indiana, had confessed to setting the fire. Brady, a cleaner and dyer with a long police record involving liquor law violations and auto thefts, had been brought to Toledo by two of Stephenson's detectives. Next day, however, Brady said his confession was a "hoax." He said he had agreed to take the blame for the fire with the understanding that he "would be taken care of." Officials ordered his release.[16]

Divided as the Indiana Klan was, with two Grand Dragons and some splinter groups, the Klan closed ranks for the

1924 elections. According to a later Stephenson deposition, he and Evans's Grand Dragon, Bossert, reached a truce in which Stephenson would run the Military Machine and Bossert would follow his orders. Though they would later be at odds in the state legislature, both the Stephenson and Evans Klan wings supported the same candidates.[17] With this arrangement, Stephenson went into the major election year of 1924 with what Stanley Frost called "the most effective political organization this country has ever seen, not excluding Tammany."[18]

6

Elections: "I Am The Law . . ."

ON NOVEMBER 4, 1924, the Knights of the Ku Klux Klan captured the government of Indiana. Determined to defend state and nation against alcohol, atheism, aliens, and the Pope, they elected a closet Klansman as governor, another as lieutenant-governor, and still another as secretary of state. Klansmen won a commanding majority in the state legislature. Klan favorites won all but one of Indiana's U.S. congressional seats.

In counties, cities, and towns across the state, Klan sheriffs, mayors, city council members, magistrates and constables were elected or already in office. And soon Grand Dragon Stephenson would be saying, with considerable justification, "I am the law in Indiana."

Nearly all of the Klan winners were Republicans. Few if any had publicly mentioned the Klan. To a casual, uninformed visitor it all might have seemed like just another part of the Coolidge landslide in that presidential election year. But the Klan victory had been pinned down many months earlier, in the May primary elections and state party convention, when Stephenson and his Military Machine had packed the Republican ticket with Klan and pro-Klan candidates.

Some newspapers had called the Republican state convention in Indianapolis a kloncilium. Much later, the *Indianapolis Times* in a review of Stephenson's career would say, "He stalked through the Republican State Convention, a revolver strapped to his side, dictating every nomination at that convention with the exception of Arthur Gilliom, now the attorney-general."[1] (There is no record that Stephenson threatened anyone with a gun. But he frequently did go armed, legally, through membership in the Horse Thief Detective Association.) Carleton McCulloch, the Democratic nominee for governor, had said shortly after the primary elections, "The Republican party has been captured by the Ku Klux Klan and has, as a political party, for the present, ceased to exist in Indiana."[2]

As the Klan-dominated Republican state convention was closing down on the afternoon of May 24, thousands of Klansmen from across the state were preparing for a huge parade through downtown Indianapolis. They had gathered during the day for a statewide rally and barbecue at the Indiana State Fairgrounds just north of the city, where Klan leaders announced the opening of a membership campaign to add 100,000 new members to the Klan's Indiana Realm.

That evening more than five-thousand Klan men and women, robed but unmasked, assembled at Sixteenth Street and proceeded south on Capitol Avenue to the downtown area, accompanied by bands, floats, and a drum and bugle corps. The procession took an hour and twenty-four minutes to pass a given point.[3] Crowds estimated at seventy-five thousand assembled to watch the parade. Except for three false fire alarms, there were no interruptions. At several points the marchers were greeted with cheers. There were no partisan political placards or displays. The *Indianapolis Star* reported that "the Klansmen marched silently, with folded arms, looking neither to the right or left." But the timing of the state rally and parade had obviously strong political overtones. Earlier in the day speakers at the fairgrounds had urged Klansmen to support

A crack Klan precision marching drill team forms a cross. (Indiana State Library)

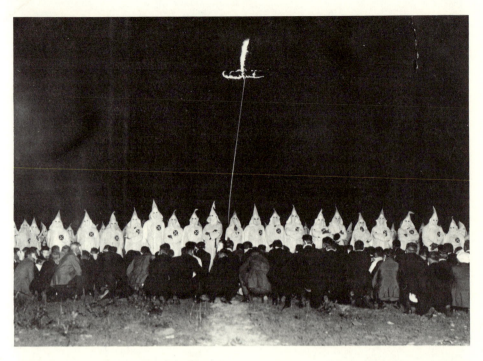

New members of the revived Klan being sworn in at South Mountain, near Brunswick, Maryland, 28 June 1922. (Culver Pictures)

EVANSVILLE HOMECOMING CELEBRATION and PICNIC

MESKER PARK
Saturday JULY 14 *All Day*

Given under auspices of Knights of the Ku Klux Klan

Evansville Klan No. 1
"The Klan That Blazed the Trail in Indiana"

Speakers, Food, Bands, and Entertainment for All

The White Gentile Protestant People of
Indiana and the Tri-State Territory
Are Cordially Invited

"Let's Go, Boy—Down by the Ohio"

14. *The Fiery Cross:* Friday, July 6, 1923.

Flyer advertising the homecoming celebration and picnic organized by the Klan for "The White Gentile Protestant People of Indiana."

David C. Stephenson, Grand Dragon of the Klan's Indiana Realm, and Klan organizer in twenty-one other northern states, looking typically confident and pleased with himself.

Dr. Hiram W. Evans, Imperial Wizard of the Knights of the Ku Klux Klan, 1926. He and Stephenson fought for control of the Klan, and the United States won when both of them lost. (A.P./Wide World Photo)

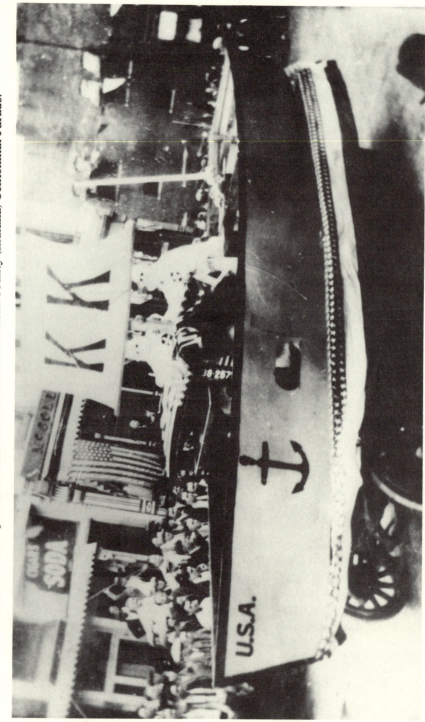

Everyone loves a parade! A Klan float in the 1923 Johnson County (Indiana) Centennial Parade.

Klansmen frequently contributed to Protestant church services. Here a group of them leave the Christian Church in Knox, Indiana after a typical visit. (Indiana State Library)

The March on Washington. Some
40,000 Klansmen and women parade
past the Capitol on Saturday, 8 August
1925. To obtain a federal permit, they
were required to march without the
usual hoods and masks. (Library of
Congress)

Ed Jackson, governor of Indiana in 1925.
He was Stephenson's choice for the state's
top executive post, and was supported by
the Klan.

Jackson for governor and "put over their men" in other coming contests across the state.

The general election in November was almost an anticlimax. At the top of the list of winners was Jackson, Stephenson's choice for governor. Jackson had a long record of dealings with the Klan. He had earlier been re-elected as secretary of state with Klan backing. In that office he had issued the charter, or permit, for the Klan (an "Atlanta corporation") to operate in Indiana. Much later a grand jury investigation would reveal that in 1923 he had conspired with Stephenson in an unsuccessful attempt to bribe the Indiana governor, Warren T. McCray, with ten-thousand dollars of Klan money if he would appoint a Klan attorney to fill a vacancy as Marion County prosecutor.

Stephenson later told grand jury investigators that he spent at least seventy-three thousand dollars on Jackson's primary campaign and more on the general election, including a Stephenson Cadillac and chauffeur and unlimited hotel expenses. Shortly before the May primary election he sent out more than 225,000 letters on Jackson's behalf to Klansmen down the line, signed simply "The Old Man." In one he praised Jackson as a "clean upright, Christian gentleman, and a man whose patriotic devotion was manifested by offering to back up with his body and his life if necessary his patriotic convictions when he enlisted in the war."

In another, "The Old Man" said, "The bootlegger, the criminal and the shyster have resorted to every resource of treachery, falsehood and double-dealing to defeat our program. But God still reigns in heaven—we can't fail. . . . We are not interested in Ed Jackson because he happens to be a Republican, but because he is a Christian gentleman and a good citizen who loves his country and his God."[4]

Except for bootleggers, there was no mention of the groups that scared and obsessed the mass of rank-and-file Klansmen—the pope and his Catholic legions, international Jewry, Bolsheviks, uppity niggers. There didn't have to be. Others had done this work for him. If The Old Man

wanted Jackson, he filled the bill. God and patriotism and
Christian morality to Klan minds meant the same thing as
defense against the pope and Jewish plots and alien forces.

While the Klan did not flaunt the Catholic issue in top
state races, it was pressed at the local level in special slates
distributed by Klansmen concerning county and town offices. For example, in Marion County's Center Township
races, one Klan-edited sample ballot excerpt is headed:
"What you have not been told about Center Township
ticket." Republican and Democratic candidates for trustee,
assessor, justice of the peace, and constable are listed side
by side.

Beneath each of the Democrats' names is inserted the
word "Catholic." Each Republican is identified as a member
of a Masonic Order: Mason, Eastern Star, or Shriner. A
footnote reminds voters that the trustee "employs all township school teachers," and that the assessor "puts the valu-
ation on your property." The justice of the peace is "the
only township judge," and the constable is "the only arrest-
ing officer."

Jackson's main rival in the Republican primary was
Mayor Samuel Lewis Shank of Indianapolis. Shank was
generally regarded as anti-Klan. But in a speech in Evansville in January 1924 he had said, "I'll not make the Klan
an issue in this campaign. I'll not make Prohibition an
issue, but I'll insist that the Prohibition law be enforced
among the rich as well as the poor."[5]

Still, the Klan was hard to avoid. Shank, a cigar-puffing,
one-time vaudeville actor had long been regarded as immoral by pro-Klan preachers, including the Reverend
Charles Gunsolus, who had told his south side Garfield
Christian Church congregation that Shank had proved
himself to be more interested in "horse racing and prize
fighting than in the higher, more elevating things of life."
The Reverend Gunsolus assailed Shank's support of "public
dancing" as "immoral," and went on to praise the Ku Klux
Klan because "it stands by the Bible, the Constitution and

the flag."[6] Shank was also repeatedly attacked in the *Fiery Cross* at Stephenson's editorial direction. He was accused of "laxity in law enforcement," with implications that bootlegging was flourishing as a result.

Shank was swamped by Stephenson's Military Machine. He got only 94,534 votes to Jackson's 224,973. State ticket choices in the primary elections still had to be ratified for formal nomination at the state party convention, but there was clearly no contest here. With Jackson, the convention proceeded to ratify and nominate such Klan favorites as F. Harold Van Orman of Evansville for lieutenant-governor, and Frederick Schortemeier for secretary of state.

With his battery of telephones in Indianapolis and direct lines to key Klan officers in every county across the state, Stephenson held a tight rein on the candidate selection process in spring 1924. Local Klan political committees approved candidates, but he could tell them what to do.

Aspiring Klan candidates for local and district offices first had to write a letter to their local Exalted Cyclops and the Klan political committee. Knowing Jackson was Stephenson's favorite for governor, many simply tied themselves to Jackson's coattails. For example, a Klansman named W. T. Quillen wanted to run for state senator from Marion County, in the Indianapolis area. He sent a letter, dated March 13, 1924, to Grover A. Smith, Exalted Cyclops of the Marion County Klan: "This to advise the election committee of my candidacy for State Senator from Marion County, subject to the Republican primaries of May 6. My platform can be said to be made up of one plank, and that plank is this: I agree, if nominated and elected, to support the program of our next governor, Ed Jackson." He said it would avail the Klan little to elect Jackson and not at the same time put people in the general assembly who would support him. He said he stood "pledged heart and soul to the principles of our organization," and that he sought this office not with the thought of any selfish gain but to the end that it will enable me to contribute to the promotion of those principles."[7]

105

During Attorney-General Gilliom's investigation of the Klan nearly four years later, Stephenson was asked if this was a typical letter. Stephenson said yes, except for its "mildness." Usually, he said, the letter "carries a pledge to appoint officials supported by the Klan." Asked about the procedure from there on, Stephenson said the political committee considers the letter and makes its decision. Then, "provided the name of the candidate is endorsed by the [Klan] political committee . . . it is given to what is called the Military Machine, together with the endorsement of the political committee. . . . The endorsements of the political committee and the Exalted Cyclops are [then] passed out through this military organization to the membership."[8] In such ways, a powerful but shadowy organization, using the Republican party as a vehicle, took control of the government of Indiana in 1924.

When an uncertain appointment, not an election, was at stake, with no Military Machine to control voters and no Klan pledges to be honored, Stephenson used money to try to get his way. In late 1923 he saw, or thought he saw, a chance to capture the Marion County prosecutor's office in this way. Republican Governor McCray was under indictment by a Marion County grand jury in Indianapolis for embezzlement and larceny of state funds. Among other things, he was charged with getting favorable private loans from several state banks in exchange for transferring to them a larger share of state deposits. Before the indictment the Marion County prosecutor had been McCray's new son-in-law, William P. Evans. Evans had resigned.

Now, Stephenson thought, McCray will be an easy target. Through Jackson, then secretary of state, he offered the governor ten-thousand dollars in Klan money if he would appoint Klan attorney James E. McDonald to fill the vacancy. McCray was also promised that he would "not be convicted by any [possibly fixed?] jury" in his forthcoming trial for illegal use of state funds. McCray refused, saying he had already decided to appoint William Remy, a stalwart and incorruptible young man then serving as a deputy prosecutor. More than three years later, at Jackson's trial for bribery, McCray, then paroled from the Atlanta penitentiary, said he had told Jackson: "It looks like I have lost my fortune I strived 20 years to make, and my office, and my liberty, but I am not going to surrender my self-respect."[9]

No deal was made. Nevertheless, McCray's Marion County embezzlement trial ended in a deadlocked jury. State charges were dropped. The case moved to federal court, where McCray was convicted of using the mails to defraud and sentenced to ten years in prison.

Despite his financial troubles, McCray basically proved himself to be a man of decency and principles. As he left for the Atlanta Federal Penitentiary in early 1924, he said: "I still maintain with a clear conscience that I am absolutely innocent of any intent to do wrong. But I'll go down there and take my medicine like a man. I believe in the courts and the enforcement of the law, and whatever the courts require I will do."[10] McCray was paroled from Atlanta on August 31, 1927. Back in Indiana, friends raised money to help him regain control of his farm. In 1929 his portrait was restored to the Governor's office in the Indiana Statehouse.

Despite the covert election year truce between Indiana's rival Klan leaders, Stephenson, in spring 1924, said he had resigned from the Klan, but he meant the national, Atlanta-controlled Klan. On May 12, between the primary elections and state convention, he called a meeting of Klan delegates from ninety-one Indiana counties in Indianapolis's Cadle Tabernacle and had himself elected new Grand Dragon of an autonomous Indiana Klan independent of "southern rule." He drew wild applause when he challenged potential political opponents of the Klan by saying, "God help the man who issues a declaration of war against the Ku Klux Klan now!"

Along with Stephenson as their Grand Dragon, the Indiana Klansmen elected a new slate of Klan officers. Earl Sigmon, an Indianapolis coal merchant, was chosen Grand

Klaliff. M. L. White, an Indianapolis dentist, became Grand Night Hawk. Among other new officers were three Protestant ministers: The Reverend H. H. Farrell of Frankfort became Grand Kludd (chief chaplain). The Reverend G. Stanley West of Brazil was elected Grand Kligrapp (secretary), and the Reverend Harry Pfeiffer of Connersville was chosen Grand Klabee (treasurer). As the voting concluded Stephenson said, "We're going to Klux Indiana as she's never been Kluxed before!"[11]

A little more than two weeks later he sought to dispel the image of Klan bigotry and shift it to the "southern crowd." He issued a public statement saying, "The Indiana Klan is not anti-Catholic nor anti-Jew, and is absolutely opposed to the program of hate and crime as promulgated by the national body in the South. The Indiana Klan, as led by me, is absolutely divorced from the national Klan as headed by Dr. H. W. Evans and Walter Bossert. Our two objectives are militant patriotism and operative religion." At the same time he explained that "operative religion" did not mean the church as a political machine, only as an effective moral force. He said he was opposed to any religious body setting itself up as a political organization, such as the Baptist church in Texas, Evans's native state, where, he claimed, one had to be a Baptist to get elected.[12]

The Klan not anti-Catholic? Baptists a problem? At first glance it might seem like an abrupt turnaround. Actually the statement was a masterpiece of demagoguery. Stephenson had often said he was not a bigot, and he may not have been. But he knew how to use other people's bigotries, and had used them, to get power and money. At the same time, however, he knew that Indiana Klansmen did not like to think of themselves as part of a hate group against individual Catholics, especially neighbors and other townspeople. They saw themselves as patriots defending America against the designs of a foreign Pope and his "pagan papist priests." More importantly, Stephenson by now had national political ambitions. He realized that he could hardly run for national office as a religious bigot, or a spokesman for an organization that preached bigotry.

Here, in one brief statement, Stephenson had supported the Klansmen's basic antipapist fears and prejudices and still made them feel noble about the whole thing. He transferred the hate-and-violence image to the "southern crowd." At the same time he had come out against churches as political organizations. Texas Baptists were not Indiana Baptists in this respect, and if they had taken political control in Texas it was a warning that a Catholic hierarchy was trying to do the same thing in Indiana.

Stephenson's efforts to erase the anti-Catholic public image of the Klan apparently extended into his editorial policies for the *Fiery Cross*, when he took control of it in 1923. Edgar Allen Booth tells of a discussion he had with one of the paper's writers; identified by the pseudonym "Wingfoot."

"You do not say anything against Catholics?" Booth asked. "Why I read it every week and—"

"And you just *think* we say something about them," the writer said. "Try to find anything like that in the paper since Steve took control. I know that here and there the word Catholic may appear, but all of the raving done in *The Fiery Cross* is about aliens, organized opposition [to the Klan] and the amalgamated enemies of America. . . ." Booth continued:

> Three weeks ago I went to Lafayette for a story. The city had an alley vacated and had given it to a Roman Catholic institute. Mayor Durgan, you know, has always played with the Catholics. . . . Klansmen there are up in arms. Well, I got a good story and returned to the office. I told Steve the members of the organization demanded that *The Fiery Cross* run the story. Steve said, 'alright, run the story but say "aliens instead of Catholics." The story did not appear, and Wingfoot said "you can't blame Lafayette Klansmen for being peeved."[13]

At the same time, however, while attempting to broaden the Klan's public appeal, no doubt for his own personal political advantage, Stephenson was apparently always ready to exploit Klan bigotry covertly for his own ends. During his fight for Klan control with Bossert, according to Booth, he encouraged rumors that Bossert's wife was Catholic, which she was not.

Further efforts to link Bossert to the Catholics were contained in a letter sent from Evansville to O. A. Shane at the Denison Hotel in Indianapolis and signed by a man named Jennings.

Shane, a wholly fictitious person, was depicted as a guest at the hotel and a prominent person in the American Unity League, an anti-Klan group composed largely of Roman Catholics. The letter said Bossert was very close to Catholic priests and the church and asked Shane to have the League work for Bossert under cover. Thousands of copies were then made and distributed to Klansmen throughout Indiana. Booth says the letter was actually written by Stephenson, who then pretended to discover it and have copies circulated.

Along with his semisecret Military Machine, Stephenson of course also wanted control of the regular, up-front Republican party machinery. Among the key grass-roots figures here were Republican county chairmen, to be elected at county conventions. The powerful heart of the Indiana Republican party was in Marion County. The county Republican chairman then was William Freeman, a city hall leader allied with Mayor Shank. Stephenson wanted to replace him with a loyal Klan captain—George Coffin. He packed the county convention with pro-Coffin delegates, and when the convention met in the criminal courtroom of the old county courthouse in May 1924, the scene resembled something out of a banana republic.

In the courthouse halls there were one-hundred armed, uniformed city police to guard the Freeman forces. In the same area there were fifty armed, uniformed deputy sheriffs to guard the Stephenson crowd. Stephenson hovered in the background, occasionally moving in and out of the offices of a friendly judge. Despite all the guns, there was

no shooting. Stephenson's man—"Cap" Coffin—won hand-
ily and stood ready to do The Old Man's bidding.

In spite of the McCray scandal in a Republican-controlled
statehouse, the Klan was still almost entirely committed to
the Republican party. A major reason was the Demon Rum,
the most obsessive issue on the Klan mind next to the pope.
The Eighteenth Amendment forbidding the manufacture
or sale of alcoholic beverages, was, in 1924, only about four
years old. But bootleggers were flourishing, and there were
already organized movements for the amendment's repeal.
The Klan, backed by churches, temperance groups, and
rural and small-town fundamentalists, was dry. And since
its Indiana beginnings in Evansville with dry Republicans
against wet Democrats, the Klan had seen the Republican
party as its ally in its proclaimed fight to destroy bootleggers and maintain Prohibition.

The pre-Prohibition saloon had been, in many ways, a
social evil. The possibility of its return stirred emotions at
least as strong as those against abortion in the 1980s. But
to many people the abuse of alcohol by some was not
sufficient reason for denying everyone a legal drink even in
his or her own home.

Some zealous "dries" seemed ready to put their lives on
the line in the cause of abstinence. Indiana's so-called Bone
Dry Law went beyond many other states in making whiskey virtually impossible to get legally, even for "medicinal
purposes." When it was revealed that Attorney-General
Gilliom, on advice of a physician, had procured bootleg
whiskey to help save the life of his sister in a Decatur
hospital, temperance groups demanded that he be prosecuted like "any other criminal." He was not prosecuted,
though a friend who got the whiskey was. The public
question posed in newspapers was: Would you violate a law
to save a life? Many said no. Mrs. Willard Gray, former
Women's Christian Temperance Union leader, said she had
had influenza during the war but made her doctor promise
not to give her whiskey, even though it was then legal. "I

would rather have died," she said, "and my opinion has not changed."[14]

Then, as now, many voters made up their minds on a single issue. Then the issue was: Was the candidate wet or dry? The Klan professed to be bone dry, and its most powerful ally was the Anti-Saloon League and its state secretary, the Reverend E. S. Shumaker. Before each election the league made up lists of its favorites and distributed them widely among church and temperance groups. Usually they coincided with the Klan favorites and added heavily to Klan strength.

In fact, the Klan and the league cooperated closely. Hugh "Pat" Emmons, one-time Exalted Cyclops in Saint Joseph County, told, during the Gilliom investigations, of a time Shumaker came to South Bend. Emmons said Shumaker asked him to bring Klan associates to his hotel room "one by one so as not to arouse suspicion." Shumaker told them, "The Klan, the Anti-Saloon League and the Horse Thief Detectives Association must work together."

In 1924, Emmons said, a man named Mike Hanley was running against Tom Goodrich for St. Joseph County sheriff. Emmons went to Shumaker and told him Hanley was a wet Catholic and Goodrich was a dry Protestant. Goodrich immediately got the League approval.[15]

Then, as now, zealots were impatient with legal processes and with courts that insisted on Constitutional rights. Law officers and Horse Thief Detectives often broke down bootleggers' doors without warning and seized evidence without search warrants. The Indiana Supreme Court overruled many convictions on grounds of illegal search and seizure. Shumaker was infuriated. In his weekly newspaper he denounced the court and finally publicly accused the judges of supporting, if not conspiring with, criminals. He was charged with contempt of court. Despite intercession of political friends, he was sentenced to sixty days on a state penal farm.

Beyond the battle zone, Prohibition had among many people become a subject for sly jokes and anecdotes. Even among those charged with enforcing the law there was often a cavalier or humorously tolerant attitude. The late Roger Williamson, one-time city hall reporter for the *Baltimore Evening Sun*, was fond of telling how he was arrested one night for having a small bottle of bootleg booze in his pocket. At the police station he was charged with illegal possession of whiskey. Next morning he appeared before a magistrate. Before he could plead one way or the other, the magistrate said: "The defendant is charged with illegal possession of whiskey. The court has examined the evidence, and in no way can this vile concoction be considered 'whiskey'. Case dismissed!"

Though he was a hero to the dry forces of Klandom, Stephenson and his cronies never went thirsty, and they didn't depend on back-alley rotgut. For the man with money there was always good whiskey filtering down from Canada, or up from rum-runners along the Florida Keys. In Indianapolis, there was also an even closer source for people with the right connections. When Prohibition went into effect, large stores of legally manufactured whiskey were still in existence. Several caches were confiscated by federal agents and placed under lock and key. One such large store was in a vault in the basement of the Federal Building in Indianapolis. The men with the keys were U.S. employees, often political appointees and some with close friends in the Stephenson crowd. Complete inventories were rarely if ever taken. Only much later was it discovered that many bottles of good pre-Prohibition whiskey had mysteriously disappeared.

Despite their smashing success in the November elections, the Republicans alienated and lost most of the traditionally Republican black vote because of the party's Klan connections. Since Abraham Lincoln's emancipation of slaves, blacks had voted almost solidly Republican. Stephenson had tried to keep it that way. One black GOP stalwart had been the publisher of the *Ledger*, W. H. Jackson—known in political circles as "Big Jack." The *Ledger* was widely circulated in the black community. Stephenson, it would later be revealed, sent at least four checks totalling more than thirteen hundred dollars to the black publisher. Stephenson's later notations on the canceled checks said they were for promotion of Ed Jackson for governor. One notation said, for example, the check was to "Big Jack, owner of the Ledger, for Jackson publicity and to be used among colored people who could be induced to work in behalf of Ed."[16]

Whatever he did it had little effect. As Moore wrote in the *Independent*:

> Politically the Klan literally drove the negro vote into the Democratic party. For the first time in the history of Indianapolis, Democratic candidates were invited to address negro rallies in the churches. A negro political parade was staged in the black belt of Indianapolis when I was there. The demonstration was spontaneous and enthusiastic. It was not pro-Democratic as much as it was anti-Republican. Banners proclaimed "Abraham Lincoln Ain't a Candidate This Year" and "Put the White Sheet on Jackson.[17]

The impact was lasting. Niblack describes a scene in 1928, when he was running for state senator on the Republican ticket:

> I saw an aged negro at a voting place in a colored precinct on Boulevard Place wearing an Al Smith [Democratic presidential candidate] button. I said, "Uncle, how can you be a Democrat after all these years?" Tears came into the good old man's eyes, and he thumped his cane on the ground and replied, "I ain't no Democrat! Don't you dare call me a Democrat! I was seventeen years old when Mr. Lincoln's boys in blue come down to Carolina and set me free, and I always been a Republican ever since." But he continued, "Let me tell you young man I'm going to vote for Mr. Al Smith. He's agin' the Klan. The Ku Klux Klan was the skunk what pissed on the Republican party in this state, and it's going to be many a long year before the stink wears off!".[18]

The open black challenge to "put the white sheet on Jackson"—an organized anti-Klan revolt in a traditional Republican enclave—was unique in the party's ranks that year. Many white Republicans were Klansmen or active Klan allies. For masses of other Republicans, the Klan was still nothing to be shunned or rejected. It still projected an image of patriotism and Christian virtue, and Klan support for their party seemed no more apt to turn them off than would support from the American Legion or the Methodist Church.

Meanwhile, Democrats facing Klansmen or Klan-backed opponents found them difficult to confront directly on the Klan issue amid the secrecy of the Invisible Empire. To be sure McCulloch, their candidate for governor, had publicly called on them to do so. In charging that the Republican party had been captured by the Klan, McCulloch had said: "The Democrats must accept the challenge and fight for the principle of religious liberty and the constitutional guaranties of the state and nation. . . . I regret the entire campaign cannot be devoted to matters of tax reductions, honesty in government, home rule and farm relief, but the Republican party has made [the Klan] the issue and we must face it squarely."[19]

This, of course, proved easier to say than to do. The Klan was an important key to Republican victory, yet it seldom if ever campaigned openly for specific candidates as Klansmen or Klan favorites, and the candidates seldom if ever mentioned the Klan. Newspapers referred to Jackson as the Klan-backed candidate for governor. The *Indianapolis Times*, in a front-page denunciation of the Klan just before the election, had said "a vote for Jackson is a vote for the Klan." But Jackson himself never mentioned the Klan publicly. In other races across the state, Democrats seemed uncertain as to whether their rivals were Klan candidates or not. Perhaps hoping for some of the Klan vote themselves, many simply avoided the issue. Klansmen, of course, knew who their friends or enemies were through their clandestine information sheets or messages from The Old Man.

At the same time, however, through the hot summer months into early fall, the Klan public presence became inescapable. Growing numbers of flaming crosses lit up night skies on hundreds of hillsides across Indiana. Increasing thousands of robed, masked men paraded through cities, towns, and villages; there were an estimated five thousand in Evansville one hot August afternoon. They carried banners supporting Protestant-Christian virtues and 100 percent Americanism. But there were no placards supporting reading Jackson for governor or Rowbottom, Stephenson's choice, for Congress.

Meanwhile, Jackson, campaigning across the state in Stephenson's Cadillac, talked in generalities: good government; fair, efficient law enforcement; equality for all citizens. He opposed "radicalism" and stood firmly for the "Constitution of state and nation." He cited his public record as secretary of state in support of these principles. He aligned himself with Calvin Coolidge, the Republican presidential candidate, and his policies of free enterprise and American sovereignty. (Coolidge himself never mentioned the Klan either. He had been "neutral," which made him favorable as compared with the Democratic candidate, John W. Davis, who was considered anti-Klan). To anti-Klan Democrats it was a frustrating experience. They knew their candidate had condemned the Klan and called for a fight against it. But how to do it? How to find individual targets in specific races if none of your opponents talked about it?

This murky situation has been described by William E. Wilson of Evansville, son of an anti-Klan congressman—also named William Wilson—running for re-election that year: "On the subject of the Ku Klux Klan a strange silence prevailed everywhere that summer, and you could not be sure whether your friends were members of the Invisible Empire or not. . . . In the main the politicians, too, were silent. Those who were opposed by the Klan were never

116

sure exactly where, what, or whom to attack because of the general animosity of their enemies."[20]

To be sure, McCulloch had denounced the Klan in general terms, as did many delegates to the Democratic National Convention in New York, which came within one vote of a platform plank condemning the Klan by name before nominating Davis for president. "But such denunciations and remarks were ignored by the Republicans," Wilson's son wrote, "and opponents of the Klan, among them my father, found themselves boxing with shadows. As for the people who would do the voting in November, they simply weren't talking." (At their national convention in Cleveland, the Republicans had sidestepped the Klan issue entirely, while nominating the "neutral" Calvin Coolidge.)

The Klan was supporting Harry Rowbottom, Congressman Wilson's Republican opponent. Whether Rowbottom was actually a member of the Klan or not was a question that couldn't be answered. No one except a few Klan officials publicly acknowledged membership. William Wilson said his father was "not an orator and, for the most part, hammered methodically at the issues." He advocated a badly needed program of flood control along the Ohio River. Although he did not drink he was opposed to Prohibition. He was an old-fashioned, low-tariff Democrat and a supporter of the graduated income tax, then still a relatively new experiment in revenue gathering.

"But," William Wilson wrote, "it was almost impossible to make the Klan an issue. . . . With no focal point for attack in the shadows of the Invisible Empire save a few acknowledged leaders and organizers, he could speak only in generalities on the subject of tolerance and decency, asserting his contempt for the forces that worked in secret against him."

In the midst of this political secrecy, however, the Klan itself became ever more visible. It was county fair time in late summer, and the Klan took over with a Konklave (a gathering) at many of them. At New Harmony, Klansmen publicly initiated a class of three hundred new members on

117

the fairgrounds. At Boonville some three-thousand robed and hooded Klansmen gathered to hear speeches about the need for 100 percent Americans to take control of things, while an airplane circled overhead dragging a twenty-foot cross through the sky. In Evansville, the Klan took out full-page newspaper advertisements for its rallies. Thousands paraded on horseback, in cars, and on foot. Women and children, all in hooded robes, some carrying flaming crosses on long poles, also paraded.

While most politicians tried to side-step the Klan issue, less than a week before the November general election the *Indianapolis Times* published a scathing denunciation of the Klan and Jackson, in oversized type, on its front page:

THE TIMES IS ANTI-KLAN

A government of the people, by the people, and for the people—

OR

A government of the people by the Klan and for the Klan.
That's the issue in next Tuesday's Indiana election.
It overshadows all other issues.
Party lines are fading.
No longer is it—are you a Democrat or a Republican or an
    independent—but instead, are you Klan or anti-Klan?
The Times wants no misunderstanding as to its attitude.
Accordingly it is herewith printing in type that you can read
    while you run—

THE TIMES IS ANTI-KLAN

The Times did not make this the issue.
The Klan made it.
But the Times accepts it.
The Times believes in government by majority—not in gov-
    ernment by minority.
The Ku Klux Klan stands for government by minority—and
    self-chosen minority at that.
The Times does not believe any secret society should be
    permitted to become Indiana's super-government.

118

It believes that a Kleagle or a Kludd or a Konclave, sitting
behind a screen, should not be allowed to steer the ship of
state.

That's why the Times is against the Klan.

A vote for Jackson is a vote for the Klan.

A vote for McCulloch is a vote against the Klan.

That's the alignment for Tuesday next—and all else is
incidental.[21]

The *Times* lost—not only the election, but circulation.

When it was all over, Jackson had defeated McCulloch
for governor by a vote of 703,042 to 492,245. William
Wilson's once-popular father had lost his seat in Congress.
Across the state, most other candidates had gone down to
similar defeat by Klan-backed opponents. Two notable Republican exceptions were Remy, who broke through the
Klan endorsement system to win election as Marion County
prosecutor, and Arthur Gilliom, who was elected Indiana
attorney-general. Remy would later prosecute Stephenson
for murder, and Gilliom's investigations would reveal much
Klan skulduggery.

But this was still to come. By the time Jackson was
inaugurated as governor on January 12, 1925, Irving Leibowitz wrote, "the invisible empire of the Klan controlled
the state of Indiana. It made the laws and enforced them.
Besides Jackson it had elected legislators, prosecutors,
judges and mayors. Nearly 500,000 Hoosiers [no doubt an
overestimate] in white robes and hoods burned their fiery
crosses almost nightly."[22]

What all this meant in human terms to anti-Klan candidates and their families has been well described by William
Wilson. He had come home to Evansville on vacation from
his first year at Harvard in summer 1924, when his father
was running for his second term in the U.S. House of
Representatives. After his first supper with his family he
went over to renew acquaintance with a longtime friend,
Link Patterson.[23] But somehow things didn't seem the
same.[24]

The Link Patterson who met me on his front porch was not the Link Patterson I remembered. . . . He looked the same and greeted me in the same old way, by cracking me hard on the biceps with his fist. . . . But he was not the old Link Patterson.

Nor were his parents the same. I had loved his mother almost as much as my own, and his father—garrulous, bawdy, and uninhibited—had always given me a man-to-man feeling that I had never shared with my own more dignified father. But that night Mrs. Patterson was restrained and formal and seemed only half-glad to see me, and Mr. Patterson said almost nothing at all. I remember especially how they watched me, as if they were waiting to accuse me of something that they knew about but I did not.

After a bit of small talk on the front porch Link got up and said he was sorry but "Mom and Dad and I have to be somewhere at eight o'clock." William left, disappointed and puzzled. Back home, his mother said the Pattersons probably only seemed different because he had been away so long. Then his father invited him to go along on a trip downtown.

On the way they approached a large vacant lot, where a fiddlers' contest and barbecue were in progress and a large crowd had gathered. "That's probably where the Pattersons are tonight," the congressman said. "The Agoga [Baptist] Bible Class is raising money to build a new Tabernacle on that lot."

"But the Pattersons aren't Baptists," William said.

"Those aren't all Baptists, by any means," his father said.

"There aren't that many Baptists in Vanderburgh County."

William asked if they were going to stop, as they frequently did at such gatherings during campaign time. His father said no.

"I'm afraid it wouldn't do any good, Harry Rowbottom has priority on that crowd."

William's father parked the car on Main Street and went into his office. When he came back he didn't start the motor but sat in silence for a couple of minutes. Finally he said, "Son, I'm not going to be re-elected in the fall."

"You're joking," William said.

The congressman shook his head. "A lot of people have turned against me. A lot of good, honest, but misguided people, like your friends, the Pattersons."

"Why, Dad, you can't help winning," William said, "As many Republicans vote for you as Democrats. You've always said that yourself. And there are all those things you've done in your first term—the Ohio River Bridge and the tax bill you wrote with Mr. Garner."

"It isn't what I've done that counts, the Congressman said. "It's what I haven't done."

"What is that?"

"Join the Ku Klux Klan."

William said that was silly. "A man like you isn't going to dress up in a sheet and make a fool of himself."

His father shook his head again. "It's a very serious matter out here this year. Senator Ralston warned me about it when he came back [to Washington, D.C.] after a trip to Indiana last Christmas, and when I came out here in the spring for the primary. I was told to join the Klan *or else*. I refused, of course, and now they're out to beat me if they have to steal votes to do it. . . . This summer is going to be an ugly business son."

Congressman Wilson nodded toward the Saturday night crowds on the sidewalk. "Too many of them have been bulldozed into a sense of self-righteousness by a bunch of demagogues. We've gone a long way in this country, but apparently still haven't freed men and women of their suspicion of each other, their prejudices, their intolerance. I think that this is going to be the big battle of this century. My little fight here in Indiana is just a preliminary skirmish and my practical political sense tells me I'm going to lose it. I'm not a crusader by nature, but, God help me, I'm not going to budge one inch from where I stand!"

The congressman was a man who gesticulated with vigor while he talked. Now, William recalls, "he clenched his fist and drove it into the windshield before him, breaking a 'V' in the glass and cutting his hand."

When William took a summer job at a gasoline filling station the Klan shadow loomed again. When he first reported for work, after being hired by the downtown office of an oil company, the station manager looked him over and said "College boy, ain't you?"

"Yes, sir," William said.

"What's your name?"

"Bill Wilson."

"Wilson? You the Congressman's son?"

"Yes, sir."

Another man came up. "Here's your new helper, Dave. We got the Congressman's son."

Dave seemed a bit friendlier, but he soon asked, "Are you a crossback, kid?"

"A what?"

"Catholic."

"No, why?"

"I heard your old man was one."

"Well, he isn't, but what difference would it make?"

"We don't want no crossbacks or kikes around here," Dave said. "Politics is different. Nobody's a Democrat or Republican anymore. Hell, I used to be a Democrat myself."

The station was on the edge of Evansville's black district. About an hour after William started work the first black customer, in a Ford truck with "hauling" printed crudely on its side, drove up. While Dave filled the tank William cleaned the windshield and filled the radiator.

As the black man left, the manager came storming out and shouted at William. "What the hell did you mean, doing that? . . . You a Bolshevik or something?"

William said he didn't understand.

"Oh yes you do!" the manager shouted. "You know damn well what I mean. Giving that nigger radiator service and wiping off his windshield."

"But you said . . ."

"I never said you was to give free service to a goddam black nigger. There ain't no job in this country can make a white man wait on a nigger. This is still a free country and you'd better learn that pretty quick—you and your old man both!"

At the mention of his father, William lost his temper. "If it's a free country, then the Negro should get the same service as everybody else."

"The *Neegro!*" the manager mocked. "Listen to him talk, will you? The *Neegro!*" He stomped angrily away.

Despite the tension, William stayed on the job all summer. He thought the manager had probably tried to fire him, but that friends of his father in the downtown office had come to his aid.

Meanwhile, he partially renewed his relationship with the Pattersons. But while Mr. Patterson was a Democrat and had supported his father ardently in 1922, he never mentioned the campaign now. "It was a strange contrast to the campaign of two years before," William recalls, when he and Link had gone to rallies for Congressman Wilson. "Now whenever I suggested going to a rally he always had something else to do."

No fiery crosses burned in the Wilson's yard. But they often burned on hillsides near the site of Congressman Wilson's campaign speeches. And soon the family began getting anonymous telephone calls. They usually began with "Hi, nigger-lover," and thereafter were unprintably obscene. There were also anonymous letters in Congressman Wilson's mail: "threats, innuendoes, scurrilous abuse, obscenities." The congressman never talked about them and William discovered them only years later in the back of a safe deposit box at the bank. He didn't know why his father had kept them. Perhaps they had been shoved to the back and forgotten. There were petty annoyances. Air let out of the tires of the family automobile. Its battery disconnected. Light bulbs unscrewed in the garage so they wouldn't respond to a switch. Window screens soaped with "KKK" initials.

On the last day before he returned to college, William stopped over to say good-bye to the Pattersons. It was "an awkward, stilted farewell," he recalls. "Link said write. Mrs. Patterson said be a good boy. Mr. Patterson said 'don't do anything I wouldn't do.' "

The Pattersons had never mentioned the Klan. But at the very last, as William was going across the porch, Mr. Patterson pushed Link aside and followed William down to the sidewalk.

"There he moved close and, holding up three fingers between his face and mine, said, 'Tell your dad it's not too late.' That was all he said. But I knew what he meant. Those three fingers were for the three K's. I didn't tell my father. I knew he would not change and I didn't want him to."

Congressman Wilson lost to Rowbottom by thirty-five hundred votes. Later, during a 1927 investigation of the Klan, it would be revealed that Rowbottom had made a written promise to Stephenson to let Stephenson control his patronage jobs. William was back at Harvard when the returns came in but talked with his family on the telephone. His mother and sister were tearful. But his father said in a strong voice, "Next time, son. Next time." He was overoptimistic. He was defeated again in 1926, and two years later, when the Klan had virtually collapsed, he had to step aside for younger men in his party.

"But that morning in the fall of 1924," William recalls, "my father's voice on the telephone gave me the confidence and courage I needed. I knew that as long as there were men like him in Indiana the Ku Klux Klan would pass."

7

A Two-Klan Legislature

WHEN THE INDIANA General Assembly convened in Indianapolis on January 8, 1925, Klansmen across the state were looking forward to a new Americanization program. Now, after long months of rallies, parades, cross burnings, and secret manipulations, it was their legislature.

Republicans were in the vast majority—eighty-two to only eighteen Democrats in the House of Representatives, thirty-two to another eighteen Democrats in the Senate. Of the Republicans, almost all were Klansmen or allies of the Klan. From Marion County alone, ten of the twelve representatives in the House were known Klan members.

They had come with a mission. "The Klan members of the 1925 legislature," said Niblack, who covered the session as a reporter for the *Indianapolis Times,* "felt a need to reform the morals of a decadent era, to inculcate patriotism, and to rescue Indiana from the clutches of the Pope and his Catholic legions."[1]

Their first targets were the Catholic schools and Catholic teachers. Among the so-called Klan bills passed by the House were:

Religious Garb Bill. This would have prevented anyone who

wore any items of religious clothing or vestments from teaching in the public schools. It was aimed especially at Catholic nuns who were teaching in Dubois, Spencer, Perry, Crawford, Floyd, and parts of Dearborn and Martin counties.

Public School Graduate Bill. This would have required that only graduates of public schools in Indiana or other states be licensed to teach in Indiana. It would have automatically eliminated Catholic school or other private school graduates.

Uniform Textbook Bill. Under this measure, Catholic as well as other parochial and private schools would be required to adopt the same textbooks as those used in the public school system.

Bible Reading Bill. This would have required that the Bible be read each day in the state's public schools without comment from the reader.

Released Time Bill. This would have permitted schools of higher learning to allow students to elect and get credit for Bible study in schools conducted by organizations outside the school system (two hours a week off if 40 percent of the parents involved requested it).

Still another bill would require students of all Indiana schools, Catholic, private or public, to study the U.S. Constitution, and another that U.S. flags be flown over every school building.

All passed the House, but none, except for the bills requiring reading of the Constitution and flying of flags at schools, became law.[2] The reason, ironically, was Stephenson.

Despite its divisions, the Klan had closed ranks for the 1924 elections. But when the legislature convened, two Klan factions were locked in a power struggle: Grand Dragon Stephenson's insurgent Indiana Klan, and the Atlanta-controlled Klan of Imperial Wizard Evans, now led by another Grand Dragon, Bossert. The Evans-Bossert forces had a majority in the House; Stephenson controlled the Senate. As Norman Weaver wrote:

> When the vote on these [House] bills came, Stephenson controlled the Senate and killed each one. Stephenson probably did not dislike them nor disapprove of their principles, but he found them too controversial. He was after other specific legislation. . . . These bills would have caused bitterness had they been passed and some of the support Stephenson wanted on other issues would have evaporated had his Klan supporters approved the bills.
>
> When he used his strength to kill them in the Senate, he created a power situation to his liking. His Klan followers went along with his decision to kill the Klan bills because they trusted him even when they wanted the bills to pass. And the Klan's opponents who opposed the religiously discriminatory bills swung to Stephenson's support on other issues because of his aid in this battle. It was a desirable power situation that "Steve" turned to his advantage.[3]

To crack down on the Demon Rum, the legislature passed what newspapers called the "Bone-Dry bill." Fines for possession or sale of intoxicating liquors were increased. On first offense, a drunken driver was charged with a misdemeanor, on the second a felony. Railroad conductors or passenger agents were given authority to arrest anyone transporting, drinking, or under the influence of liquor in their areas. Alcohol was still needed in medical work, but it was limited to pure grain, and only pharmacists with an official permit and only on special written application for each sale could purvey it. In some states, pharmacists and physicians had become conduits for booze under the medical purposes cover. The Indiana bill sought to avoid this with copious, detailed provisions for keeping and double checking written records.

A major prize on Stephenson's agenda was control of the state highway commission. Years later he told grand jury investigators that he had been promised this by Jackson in return for getting him elected governor. The potential for money and power was enormous. Automobiles were multiplying by the thousands, bringing a demand for millions of dollars in new road construction. Control of the highway commission meant control over highway building contracts. Stephenson's bill would have reorganized the commission, creating vacancies in high places. Jackson could then appoint new people, Stephenson's henchmen, to control it.

Stephenson lost this one. It became known in the newspapers as the "Road Ripper bill." It was not really a Klan issue. The highway department had some twelve hundred employees. Too many members of the legislature had connections there and didn't want to see them disturbed.

But another path to big money still lay open. After the legislative session, Stephenson planned to have Jackson appoint his choice for state purchasing agent. Among other things, Stephenson owned the Enos Coal Company in Pike County. Competitive bidding rules were more easily bypassed then. With his man as purchasing agent, Stephenson planned to get contracts to supply coal to all state institutions at his own price.

Curiously, Stephenson by then had sold his Central States Coal Company. In November 1924 he had publicly announced that he was selling the company, along with his Central Sand and Gravel Company, to his earlier partner, L. G. Julian, of Evansville, for $200,000. He said he had accepted a position as general manager of a New York firm at $25,000 a year, but did not wish to give the name of the company at that time.

It was apparently a move to get Julian out of the act and give himself sole control of the state coal business under another aegis. According to the *Indianapolis News* of November 11, 1924, he said he had caused to be written into the contract for the sale of the two companies to Julian a provision that the companies could not sell their products to the state during the term of the next governor. Whatever Stephenson's plan was, it never had a chance to materialize. By the time he had hoped to implement it, he was in jail without bond, charged with murder.

Still, the 1925 legislature had been in many ways a gold

mine for Stephenson. So far as is known, he never personally set foot in the legislative halls during the session. But his offices in the Kresge building in downtown Indianapolis, which he continued to maintain after the coal company sale, were only about four blocks away from the capitol. Legislative leaders came regularly to these offices for instructions, while special interest groups stood by with lobbying money. Leibowitz said "utilities, trade organizations, and business groups came to him (usually with money) to get their bills passed into law."[4] "Stephenson," Norman Weaver said, "made a real stake by selling influence during this session of the legislature. In addition, he wielded the power he so coveted. He got what he wanted in most cases."[5]

He had proved he could get Klansmen to vote no when they wanted to vote yes. The Bible-reading bill was passed three times in different forms by the House and defeated in the Senate each time. He had stymied the Evans-Bossert forces. He was also, he thought, well on his way to almost total personal control of the government of Indianapolis. His choice for mayor, Klansman John Duvall, had already made promises to take his orders, as had six Klansmen who were running for the city council. All looked favorable. All would later be elected in the municipal balloting of November 1925.

Despite Klan in-fighting, the 1925 Indiana legislature had some notable accomplishments on its record. Among other things, it passed a bill creating the present spacious and resource-rich state library and historical department. It prohibited the sale of unpasteurized milk, authorized purchase of the Indiana Dental College by Indiana University, and created the Marion County Municipal Court, a reform measure sponsored by the Indianapolis Bar Association.

Stephenson's ambitions went far beyond Indiana. He had been a King Kleagle in Ohio and a Klan propagation chief in some twenty other northern states. He had traveled widely and spoken to Klansmen throughout the Middle

West. Edgar Allen Booth—then a close associate of Stephenson—recalled that as early as 1923 "his active and crafty brain had already realized the power he wielded through the hundreds of staunch followers he had now gained in the Central States. Already in Indiana, Ohio, Illinois and Michigan politicians were beginning to cast about for favor in the eyes of Stephenson".

"Stephenson began to picture himself in the White House," Booth says. "Visions of a Mussolini in America floated before him. In his fervid brain it began to be only a matter of time until he was a dictator—not only in the Klan but in the United States."[6] A bust of Napoleon adorned his desk in Indianapolis. Benito Mussolini, Italy's Fascist dictator, was known to be one of his idols. He had followed Il Duce's rise to power in Italy with fascination: first, a Socialist editor and leader; then strikes and bloody rioting; then Mussolini's turn-about drive against the "Reds," with himself and his *Fascisti* as the saviors of the nation from its chaos.

In 1923, Booth says, Stephenson believed the time was ripe for some sort of widespread revolutionary chaos in the United States. At least some facts supported his wilder imaginings. Over-worked and under-paid factory workers and miners were fighting to organize unions and bargain collectively against powerful union-busting, sometimes violent industries. Strikes were often bloody. In mid-1922, thirty-six coal miners had been killed in a strike battle at Herrin, Illinois. Midwestern farmers were hard-pressed financially. Anti-Wall Street, agrarian Populism was spreading, a new Farmer-Labor Party was growing, along with increasingly active Socialist and Socialist-labor parties.

The foremost champion of reform was the veteran Wisconsin senator, Robert M. LaFollette, Jr. ("Fighting Bob"), a maverick Republican turned Progressive. LaFollette was widely regarded by the vested interests as a radical, if not a Bolshevik, but it was generally expected that he would be a strong third-party candidate for president in 1924.

Against this background, Booth claims, an "astounding"

plot began to ferment in Stephenson's mind, along with that of the eccentric Klansman-sculptor Gutzon Borglum, and a minor third accomplice, Edward Rumely of LaPorte, Indiana.

Borglum, at fifty-seven, was a widely acclaimed artist. His bust of Abraham Lincoln stood in the Capitol Rotunda in Washington, D.C. His figures of apostles graced the church of Saint John the Divine in New York City. By 1927 he would begin what is today a major tourist attraction—the sixty-foot-high heads of four U.S. presidents carved in stone on the side of South Dakota's Mount Rushmore. Less known then was that Borglum had been a ranking member of the Ku Klux Klan's Imperial Kloncilium and a confidante of Indiana's Grand Dragon Stephenson.

Borglum's active association with a Klan that was dominantly antialien and generally antilabor union seems curious in the light of some of his other activities. He was, for example, among many Americans who opposed the conviction of two Italian immigrant anarchists—Nicola Sacco and Bartolomeo Vanzetti—for the robbery and murder of a factory paymaster in Massachusetts in 1920. Much evidence was questionable. Many, including Borglum, felt the two had been convicted more for their political beliefs than the actual crime and, the Sacco-Vanzetti case became a national issue. After they were executed in 1927, following years of legal maneuvering and public outcries, Borglum did a small bronze bas-relief with their profiles and an inscription that reads, in part, "a lesson to the forces of freedom that our suffering and death will not have been in vain." He had hoped it would be placed in Boston, but it never was, and after his death in 1941 it mysteriously disappeared from his studio.[7]

Another of Borglum's admiring statues was of John P. Altgeld, the stormy Illinois Democratic governor widely regarded as a prolabor radical in the 1890s. Altgeld had provoked public outrage when he pardoned two labor anarchists who had been imprisoned for the Chicago Haymarket Massacre, a bombing in which seven police officers were killed in 1886. Four others accused in the bombing had been put to death, after a questionable trial by a heavily prejudiced judge and jury. Altgeld's prolabor image was further sharpened when he vigorously opposed, on constitutional grounds, the use of army troops to put down the Chicago Pullman railroad strike in 1894.

Borglum lived in Stamford, Connecticut, where Stephenson often met with him. According to Booth, their plan, or fantasy, to make Stephenson the nation's savior was this: After LaFollette's expected nomination for president on a third-party ticket in 1924 they would, without LaFollette's knowledge, swing their support to him behind the scenes. Stephenson's Klan machines would bring in the central states. Borglum would carry areas farther west, including his native Idaho, through influence with nonpartisan leagues. Together they would win enough states so that no candidate in a three-way race among top contenders would win a majority of electoral votes.

The choice of a president would then be thrown to Congress, as provided in the Constitution. While the two old parties debated, conspirators would spread the word that a plot was underway by capitalists and vested industrial interests to cheat LaFollette out of the presidency. When, as expected, LaFollette lost, they would then trumpet the charge that Wall Street and Big Money had paid off Congress to prevent the labor and agrarian reforms LaFollette was championing. This would incite radicals and Bolsheviks, soon joined by Socialists and farmer-labor groups, to widespread strikes, street violence, and bombings. In the resulting chaos Stephenson would arise as a new leader for law and order—an American Il Duce.[8]

This mad scheme, if it was ever seriously contemplated, never had a chance, of course. LaFollette was indeed nominated for president by a strong new Progressive party. In November 1924 he got nearly five million popular votes, the largest third-party percentage in U.S. history except for that of George Wallace in 1968. But it amounted to only thirteen electoral votes, against 382 for Republican Coolidge and 136 for Democrat Davis. LaFollette died in 1925, apparently never having heard of the plot described by Booth. Even before the 1924 elections, he had publicly condemned the Klan and was widely regarded by Klansmen as an enemy, making Stephenson's alleged scheme even more unpromising. And by early 1925, Stephenson and Borglum had come to a parting of the ways and Stephenson was suing Borglum for repayment of a twenty-five thousand dollar loan.

Stephenson did, in fact, inject LaFollette into the 1924 Indiana gubernatorial election. It was later revealed that he had financed the fake of a LaFollette candidate for governor to draw LaFollette-for-president voters away from the Democratic state ticket. D. W. Raymond of Valparaiso, Indiana, had used the LaFollette label in filing his candidacy by petition. The scheme was exposed by the regular LaFollette organization, and Raymond was denounced as an imposter. Stephenson said his action was instigated by Jackson and Clyde Walb, state Republican chairman.[9]

Alcohol certainly had much to do with Stephenson's overweening ambitions and political fantasies. Booth, who spent many hours with him in conversation before he finally split with the "Mad Mullah," said,

> Once in a great while, when drinking very heavily, he would talk revolution. He would pride himself that he was to lead this revolution. On one occasion in Columbus [Ohio] he became exceedingly intoxicated. He then began to curse capital and talk revolution. I remonstrated until he grew abusive, and then left him. The next morning he wanted to know what he had said to me the night before. I told him I had paid no attention to his "drunken mouthings" and he dropped the subject. Later in the day he asked me who he had mentioned in this talk of the night before. I assured him he had mentioned no names, and he hadn't, and he seemed much relieved.[10]

Drunk or not, did Stephenson really have these ideas seriously in mind? He had, it may be recalled, been a speaker for Socialist causes in his earlier years in Oklahoma. Was it some residue of these earlier commitments that had become the stuff of drunken dreams wherein a multimillionaire talked revolution and cursed capital? Booth had become an enemy of Stephenson and was out to expose him. He was probably prone to exaggerations. Nevertheless, most writers agree that Stephenson, drunk or sober, had national political ambitions. He still hoped for an appointment to fill a possible vacancy in the U.S. Senate by his governor-ally, Ed Jackson, and from there a good shot at the White House in 1928.

In any event, he never had a chance to find out if his hopes were valid. On the night of January 12, 1925, at Governor Jackson's inaugural banquet in the Indianapolis Athletic Club, he met and danced with a young woman statehouse employee named Madge Oberholtzer. She was twenty-eight years old, single, and lived with her parents in the same Irvington suburb not far from Stephenson's mansion. Her father, George Oberholtzer, worked for the railroad mail service. She had attended Butler College (later to become Butler University) and had been a rural schoolteacher and a secretary before coming to the statehouse, where she worked in a special literacy program of the state Department of Public Instruction.

Madge was not a femme fatale, but a rather plain brunette who wore her hair in the careless up-swept style of the times. She was a bit plump—5 feet, 4 inches tall and weighing about 145 pounds. She had once been engaged, but marriage plans were interrupted when her young man had to go away to war.

Stephenson had his choice of many women, but he was attracted to Madge. She was known in Irvington as a "nice girl." After her death in April 1925, the *Butler Alumnal Quarterly* published a memorial picture with a caption that read, "In loving remembrance of Madge Oberholtzer, ex. '18, who died at her house in Irvington on April 14. Pleasant in friendship, faithful in duty, of fine Christian character."[11]

134

Perhaps after the succession of hired, lacquered whores who frequented Stephenson's mansion, something in this "nice" girl stirred another facet of his sex drives. For her own part, Madge was, friends said, ambitious and attracted to important people. She obviously knew Stephenson was important. She also knew, or soon would know, that he could control bills in the state legislature—including education bills that could affect her job. Whatever the attraction for one or the other, it was the beginning of the end, in different ways, for both of them.

8

The Ides of March

IN THE WEEKS following their dance at the governor's banquet, Stephenson called Madge several times for dates. They dined at least twice at the Washington Hotel. She was among several guests at a dinner party in his mansion, only a few blocks from her home in Irvington. All were apparently decorous affairs. Stephenson called for Madge in his chauffeur-driven Cadillac and returned her to her parents' house at an early hour. The dinner party was especially impressive, attended by "several prominent people," the kind Madge liked to meet.[1]

There was little or nothing in evidence that night to indicate what the Stephenson mansion had actually become. Although its facade had been re-designed, it was, she knew, the former Kappa Kappa Gamma sorority house at the edge of the Butler College campus.[2] Stephenson had purchased it in 1923, when the sorority moved to a new location on East Washington Street. Possibly one thing that had attracted him to it was a large outdoor balcony overlooking a lawn and the street beyond. This would later be replaced with a high, mansion-like four columned entrance. But for now it was here that he could stand, Mussolinilike, to exhort assembled, robed Klansmen on the virtues of 100

percent Americanism and Christian morality. But inside—
where young coeds had once read Keats or John Donne or
waltzed to "Three O'Clock in the Morning"—bootleg booze
now flowed freely. Hired, naked women sometimes cavorted
into the wee hours. Dresser drawers were filled with loaded
pistols.

Court Asher, the Indiana bootlegger and Stephenson
crony, later talked freely of the goings-on there. One Stephenson pasttime, he said, was to play satyr to as many as
six or seven hired wood nymphs. Everyone would strip
naked. Then while the nymphs tripped about the room,
Stephenson would sit in a chair, snapping at them with a
long whip until they dropped out one by one. The lone
survivor would win a special financial reward and share his
bed for the night.[3] Neighbors had heard suspicious noises
and suspected weird things, but on the night Madge dined
there the atmosphere was genteel, as were the guests.

Soon this image would change. On Sunday night, March
15, 1925, Madge returned to her home about 10:00 P.M.,
after an afternoon and evening with friends. When her
escort left, her mother told her that someone had been
calling on the telephone from Irvington number 0492.
Madge returned the call. Stephenson answered. He told her
he was getting ready to go to Chicago and wanted to see
her on a matter of importance before he left.

Stephenson had earlier interested himself in legislation
affecting the state education department, and she apparently thought it might involve her career. He had already
killed one bill that would have cost her her job. He sent one
of his bodyguards—a burly former police officer and now
deputy sheriff named Earl Gentry—to accompany her.
They walked from Madge's house at 5802 University Avenue the short distance to Stephenson's place at 5432 University Avenue. From then on, according to Madge's statements to her parents and physicians, a sworn declaration
to her father's lawyer, and court records, this is what
happened:

As soon as she got inside Stephenson's house she saw

that he had been drinking. His housekeeper was gone. There was no other woman in the house, and she was "very much afraid." She was taken to the kitchen by Stephenson and Gentry, where they were joined by another bodyguard named Earl Klinck. There she was offered a drink. "I said I wanted no drink," she recalled, "but Stephenson and the others forced me to drink. I was afraid not to do so and I drank three small glasses of the drink [later described as drugged]. This made me ill and dazed and I vomited."

Stephenson said he wanted Madge to go to Chicago with him. She refused, but he said, "You cannot go home." Gentry and Klinck took loaded guns from a dresser drawer. Gentry called for drawing room reservations on the 1:00 A.M. Monon train for Chicago through the rail ticket desk at the Washington Hotel, where Stephenson maintained a suite. Weak and dazed from the drinks, Madge was forced into a car with the others. They drove to the Indianapolis Union Station, stopping briefly at the hotel to pick up tickets. Stephenson, Madge and Gentry boarded the train shortly before 1:00 A.M.

Once aboard, Madge said,

> They took me at once to the compartment. I cannot remember clearly everything that happened after that. I know Gentry got into the top berth of the compartment. Stephenson took hold of the bottom of my dress and pulled it up over my head. I tried to fight but was weak and unsteady. Stephenson took hold of my two hands and held them. I had not the strength to move. What I had drunk was affecting me. Stephenson took all my clothes off and pushed me into the lower berth. After the train started Stephenson got in with me and attacked me. He held me so I could not move. . . . He chewed me all over my body, bit my neck and face, chewing my tongue, chewed my breasts until they bled, my back, my legs, my ankles . . .

She said she lost consciousness, and the next thing she remembered was hearing a buzzer and the porter calling for passengers to get off the train for Hammond, Indiana, just short of the Illinois state line. In Hammond they walked to the Indiana Hotel, where Stephenson checked himself and Madge into Room 416 as "Mr. and Mrs. W. B. Morgan" of Franklin, Indiana. Gentry registered under his own name, from Indianapolis, and took the adjoining room 417. (Klinck had remained in Indianapolis.) Stephenson, now more sober, apologized for his actions of the night before. Gentry put hot towels on Madge's head and bathed her wounds with witch hazel. Meanwhile, Stephenson's chauffeur, "Shorty," had been contacted and was bringing a car from Indianapolis.

Back in Irvington, Madge's parents had retired early the night before and did not know of her continued absence until the next morning. They were disturbed when they awoke to find her still gone. But about 8:00 A.M. Madge's mother received a telegram from Hammond, dictated by Stephenson, sent by Gentry, and signed "Madge." It said, "We are driving through to Chicago. Will be home on night train."

Madge had protested the plan to go to Chicago, but Stephenson said she was going. He said he wanted to marry her. Distraught, still in some shock, and fearing for a scandal and shame on her family, she said she thought at one time of getting Stephenson's pistol and shooting herself. But when Shorty arrived she said she wanted to go out and buy a hat. (She had left home without hat or purse or other clothing besides what she wore on the walk to Stephenson's house.) Stephenson told Shorty to give her $15.00 and take her out to buy the hat, and she bought a black silk one for $12.50. Then she asked Shorty to stop at a drugstore where she could get rouge. Instead, she bought a box of eighteen bichloride of mercury tablets and put them in her pocket.

Back at the Indiana Hotel, when she thought Stephenson was asleep, she took six of the tablets. She said she couldn't take more because "they burned so." She became ill again and vomited. When Stephenson awoke a little after 4:00 P.M. and found what she had done he ordered a quart of milk and made her drink it. Then he said, "We'll take you to a hospital and you can register as my wife. Your stomach will have to be pumped out."

When Madge refused, Stephenson then said, "We'll take you home." Madge said she wanted to stay there, or to register at another hotel under her own name. Stephenson then said he wanted her to go to Crown Point, Indiana, with him and get married. Again she refused. Stephenson then told Shorty, "Pack the grips," and they headed back to Indianapolis.

License plates were removed from the car. Stephenson told Shorty to "drive fast, but don't get pinched." If anyone asked about the missing plates he should say that they had been stolen. At the hotel the men had picked up more liquor, and Stephenson and Gentry were drinking all the way.

"All the way back to Indianapolis"—a 175-mile road trip—Madge said, "I suffered great pain and screamed for a doctor. I said I wanted a hypodermic to ease the pain, but they refused to stop." She said she heard Stephenson say, "This takes guts to do this, Gentry, she is dying." She said she also heard him say he had been in a worse mess than this before and had gotten out of it. Stimulated by alcohol, Stephenson boasted of the money he had made, said he had power, and that his word "was law."

They got back to Indianapolis late that night. Madge's mother, believing the telegram, had met the night train in vain. They drove straight to Stephenson's home. Madge was carried to a loft above Stephenson's garage, where she was kept until the next morning, when she was awakened by Klinck. Klinck said, "You have to go home."

"I asked him where Stephenson was," Madge recalled, "and he said he didn't know. I remember Stephenson had told me to tell everyone I had been in an automobile accident, and he said, 'You must forget this, what has been done has been done. I am the law and the power.'"

Klinck took Madge home a little before noon on Tuesday, March 17. Her disturbed parents were away, seeking her whereabouts. Klinck carried her upstairs to her bedroom.

On the way down he met a woman who was a roomer at the Oberholtzer house, Eunice H. Schultz. She asked who he was and he said, "My name is Johnson, from Kokomo. . . . I must hurry." He said Madge had been in an auto accident. Upstairs Madge was groaning and said, "Oh, I am dying Mrs. Schultz!" When her parents got home they immediately called the family physician, Dr. John Kingsbury. He was soon joined by Mr. Oberholtzer's lawyer, Asa J. Smith.

On April 2 Madge's father swore out a criminal complaint against Stephenson, charging abduction and assault. Stephenson was arrested at his suite in the Washington Hotel by police lieutenant Jess McMurtry and three detectives.

Stephenson first told them he was "Mr. Butler" (the name of his secretary—Fred Butler). Finally he gave his real name and angrily asked, "What is this racket?" When told they had a warrant for his arrest he said, "Very well, read it." After the warrant was read, Stephenson said, "I am armed. Do you want me to disarm?" They said yes and Stephenson handed over a .45 caliber automatic pistol and a badge reading "Horse Thief Detectives Association."

At the courthouse the next day, reporters asked Stephenson about the charges. "Nothing to it," he said. "Nothing to it. I'll never be indicted." But soon a Marion County grand jury indicted not only Stephenson, but Gentry and Klinck as well, for assault and battery, malicious mayhem, kidnapping, and conspiracy. Meanwhile, Stephenson was free on twenty-five thousand dollars bail, Gentry and Klinck on five thousand dollars each.

On April 14, Madge Oberholtzer died.

On April 18, Stephenson, Gentry, and Klinck were indicted for first-degree murder. Bail was denied and all were lodged in the county jail. There were four counts in the murder indictment returned by the Marion County grand jury:

The first charged the men with kidnap-assault and refusal to get Madge an antidote for deadly poison, bichloride of mercury, which she had taken while she was kept by them in "forcible custody," whereby she died.

The second count charged that they caused her to take the poison by her own hand by putting her under duress, fear, and compulsion.

The third charged that the defendants did feloniously assault her by striking, beating, biting, and wounding her with intent to forcibly ravish and rape her, causing her to "sicken, languish and die," as a result. (At this time it was apparently still not clear that Klinck had remained in Indianapolis.)

The fourth count charged that they had kidnapped Madge; that Stephenson assaulted and bit her; that while in throes of pain, mental anguish, and distraction, she swallowed the poison; and that they refused her a physician or an antidote, and because of this she died.

The charges were based primarily on Madge's "dying declaration," which she made to her father's attorney shortly before she slipped into her final coma. By March 28, twelve days after she was attacked on the train, Dr. Kingsbury and consulting physicians were certain Madge was dying. Many of her wounds had responded to treatment, but a deep bite wound on one of her breasts had become heavily infected, with an acute pus infection and an abscess in the outer portion of the lung just below it. The doctors said this, together with the poison she had taken and the lack of prompt medical treatment, was taking its toll—nephritis and degeneration of the liver and heart.

Asa Smith, the lawyer who had talked with Madge earlier, was called again to her bedside to take her "dying declaration." Smith had prepared a detailed typewritten statement that he now read back to her slowly and carefully in the presence of three witnesses. It covered in detail Madge's description of the abduction, attack, and the events that followed. It closed with: "I, Madge Oberholtzer, am in full possession of all my mental facilities and understand what I am saying. The foregoing statements have been made to me and I have made them as my statements and they are all true. I am sure that I will not recover from this illness, and I believe that death is very near to me, and I have made all of the foregoing statements as my dying declaration and they are true." She then signed the declaration, which was to become key evidence at the murder trial.

Madge's statement that she was sure she was dying when she made the declaration was important. In the absence of direct, personal testimony from the witness stand, courts were prone to accept dying declarations as an exception to the rule against hearsay evidence. The premise was that a person about to meet his or her Maker would not lie.

Months of legal maneuvering followed. For himself and his codefendants, Stephenson had secured the services of some of the state's top legal talent. His chief counsel was Eph (for Ephraim) Inman, long regarded as one of the best criminal lawyers in the state. Standing six feet tall, with silvery hair and a flair for exploiting dramatic possibilities, Inman had an impressive record of victories in jury trials.

Inman first moved to get the defendants freed on bail. This was denied. Then he moved to have parts of the indictment stricken as unsupported by proper evidence. This too failed, after hearings in criminal court. Then he moved to have the entire indictment quashed, charging it was "ambiguous, duplicitous, indefinite, vague and uncertain." This also was denied.

Finally, when a trial became inevitable, Inman moved that the case be venued—or transferred—from Marion County to the Hamilton County Circuit Court in Noblesville, a city of about five thousand some thirty miles north of Indianapolis. He charged that the atmosphere of public hostility in Marion County had made it impossible to get an impartial jury or a fair trial there.

This was soon granted. There were ample grounds for it. In the weeks and months following Stephenson's arrest, women's clubs, community groups, and ad hoc gatherings had, in various ways, whipped up public opinion against Stephenson. One mass meeting included some five hundred residents of Irvington demanding justice for Madge's death. Butler College, where Madge had once been a student, formed a group to aid her family.

At a meeting on April 27, the Women's League at Butler adopted a resolution offering support to the Oberholtzer family and to the prosecutor's efforts to bring to justice those responsible for her death. With no mention of Stephenson, it read, in part:

> We, the members of the Women's League of Butler College . . . bear a share of the general grief in the death of Madge Oberholtzer . . . a young woman who was highly esteemed and beloved. Therefore, we wish to extend to Miss Oberholtzer's father, mother and brother our deep and sincere sympathy and to cooperate with them and our community in support of William H. Remy, prosecuting attorney, in his endeavor to bring to justice those who are responsible for this tragedy, for the immediate vindication of right and the prevention of similar crimes hereafter.[4]

The Indiana Federation of Women's Clubs meeting in West Baden on June 4 unanimously adopted resolution opposing bail for Stephenson, Klinck, and Gentry. It read:

> The Indiana Federation of Women's Clubs in session here considers the development of ideals of the American home and considers that those who hold high offices of state, county and town are sponsors of the home and are responsible for violations of the laws of the state. The women of Indiana in this convention represent thirty thousand homemakers and they demand that the enemies of the home be so dealt with that the streets may be made safe for use.
>
> Resolved, that we petition those in authority to uphold the law and the bail be denied to Stephenson, Klinck and Gentry who are now under indictment for the murder of Madge Oberholtzer.[5]

Stephenson professed to see behind much of this the hands of his enemies in the Evans-Bossert wing of the Klan. He said at least one mass meeting had been deliberately promoted by Evans and Bossert. A few Stephenson supporters tried to impugn Madge's reputation, spreading tales that she had been intimate with many men. They suggested that she had been much more familiar with Stephenson than was generally known. Significantly, however, most of Stephenson's former Klan faithful were silent. An idol had fallen even before his trial. The wound that would grow deeper and finally destroy the Klan in Indiana and much of the Middle West had already begun to fester.

Meanwhile, Stephenson's mansion in Irvington had been the target of arson. On the night of April 16–17, 1925, a fire of "incendiary origin" had swept through the big house on University Avenue. Stephenson was then still on bail just a day before he was arrested on the murder charge and living at his suite in the Washington Hotel.

Nearby residents in Irvington told firefighters they had seen flames and then heard explosions, which shattered several windows. The fire was quickly controlled, but investigators found that several cans of gasoline had been placed inside to feed the flames, and, later, in the cold ashes of the fireplace they found several unexploded 12-gauge shotgun shells.

Stephenson could hardly blame this on his enemies. In October of the same year, while facing trial for murder in Noblesville, Stephenson himself, along with Klinck, Gentry, and Stephenson's secretary, Fred Butler, was indicted in the arson case, for trying to defraud an insurance company that had a twenty-thousand-dollar policy on the Stephenson house. Further action was delayed pending the outcome of the Noblesville murder trial.

By now Stephenson's past was beginning to catch up with him. In mid-March his first wife, now Mrs. Nettie (for Jeanette) Stephenson Brehm, had arrived in Indianapolis from Poteau, Oklahoma, with her eight-year-old daughter to sue Stephenson for $16,795, charging desertion and nonsupport.

She said she had been married to Stephenson at Tishomingo, Oklahoma, on March 26, 1915, and that Stephenson had fathered her child and then deserted her and failed to provide support. Stephenson said that Mrs. Brehm's trip and lawsuit were financed by the Evans-Bossert faction of the Klan. Nevertheless, she finally won her suit for a lesser amount by default, because no attorneys appeared for Stephenson.

Whether changing the trial to Noblesville would ease the anti-Stephenson hostility soon became doubtful. Stephenson said he learned that Evans and Bossert had descended on the Hamilton County Klan, a unit that had grown rather inactive, to reorganize and rejuvenate it. He was heatedly denounced on the floor at Klan meetings in Hamilton as well as Marion County. And at a *chautauqua,* a popular traveling evangelical tent show then appearing in Hamilton County, the county Klan unit paid a reported $1,250 for a "Klan Day" at which Stephenson was again assailed.[6]

Stephenson said his life was threatened twice. One Klansman, Robert McNay, visited Stephenson in jail under a false name. Stephenson said McNay warned him that he would be shot if he dared to take the witness stand in his own defense. Years later, with Stephenson still maneuvering for release from prison, several affidavits were published testifying to the hostile atmosphere and threats on his life before and during the trial in Noblesville. One affidavit, signed October 29, 1939, was from Charles Q. Gooding, the Hamilton County sheriff, who had custody of Stephenson in the weeks before his trial.

> Sometime during the month of August, 1925, the ku klux klan held some kind of celebration in Noblesville, while David C. Stephenson was in the county jail awaiting trial. During the klan celebration large numbers of people went about the streets of Noblesville garbed in ku klux klan robes and masks. Shortly before noon (on one day) at a time when the mid-day meal was being served to the prisoners in the county jail, a large number of robed and masked men assembled around the county jail and engaged in loud, boisterous and profane shouting. Most of the robed and masked men assembled at the west side of the jail and

shouted through the windows where they could see him. The masked and robed men repeatedly told Stephenson they would kill him if he exposed klan politics or klan interest in his conviction, or that in substance.

The sheriff said he ordered the robed men to leave the jail area. In reply the men said they had come to warn Stephenson, and one said the Klansmen "would take Stephenson out of the county jail and kill him if he said anything about the klan or revealed its political secrets in his trial." Later in the day, he said, Imperial Wizard Evans spoke to a large assembly of people in the Noblesville area on a Klan Day. About 5:00 P.M. the same day, robed Klansmen again gathered on the sidewalk near the jail and again shouted threats against Stephenson's life if he revealed Klan interest in his prosecution.[7]

Another affidavit, signed December 2, 1939, was from Alfred Hogston, who had charge of Klan activities in thirty-five northern Indiana counties in 1925. Hogston said that "in the early part of August a big Klan meeting was held at Noblesville, at which Dr. Evans was present." He asked a top state Klan official, W. Lee Smith, why the meeting was held at Noblesville, and Smith said it had been arranged by Evans.

He said he made further inquiries to McNay, who was in charge of Klan units in central Indiana, and Huffington, the anti-Stephenson Klan leader from Evansville and a close associate of Evans. "McNay and Huffington," Smith said, "both told me that Dr. Evans put on the meeting in Hamilton County for the purpose of keeping Klan sentiment high in the county against D. C. Stephenson so that Stephenson would be sure to be convicted."[8]

Despite these shows of hostility, Stephenson and his codefendants lived well at the jail. The friendly old sheriff seemed convinced that Stephenson had been framed by enemies within the Klan. With the sheriff's cooperation, Stephenson had company at the jail whenever he wanted it, sometimes a woman whom he would entertain in private.

In later grand jury investigations of Klan political corruption, it was testified that certain county and state officials had provided him with money, books, specially prepared food, and liquor—some reportedly from the cache of impounded booze in the federal building basement in Indianapolis.[9]

In such a milieu, one of Indiana's longest, most-publicized, and—to many—most controversial murder trials was set to begin in the old red brick courthouse in Noblesville on October 12, 1925.

9

The Trial: Murder or Suicide?

WAS MADGE OBERHOLTZER'S DEATH murder or suicide? Did she die from self-administered poison, from infection caused by wounds inflicted on her during a sadistic assault, or a combination of both? Was she driven to take the poison by the pain and mental anguish she suffered at the hands of the defendants, and did that itself make them guilty of murder?

These were the essential questions that confronted a jury of ten farmers, a businessman, and a truck driver in the circuit court at Noblesville in October 1925. Jury selection took a full eleven days. Some four hundred veniremen had been questioned before the final twelve were chosen. The major reason for this was the public uproar over the case, especially centering on the Klan and its rebel Grand Dragon, D. C. Stephenson. It was widely suspected that many prospective jurors had been contacted and pressured by various Klansmen before they ever entered the courtroom.

Judge Will H. Sparks allowed extreme latitude to attorneys for both sides in questioning each potential juror. He allowed searching, intimate inquiries into their personal lives, business and social connections, and knowledge of the case and its principal people. Challenges eliminated any who had been suspected of membership in or support for the Klan. While all of those finally chosen had heard of Stephenson, all denied knowing him personally or having any fixed feelings about his guilt or innocence.

Presentation of the case to the jury began on October 25, The prosecution was headed by Remy, the able and stalwart Marion County prosecutor. Despite the transfer of the trial to Hamilton County, Remy had retained his position in the case for the state. He was joined by Justin A. Roberts, the Hamilton County prosecutor; Charles Cox, a sixty-five-year-old former Indiana Supreme Court Justice; and Ralph Kane, an able Indianapolis lawyer who had formerly practiced in Hamilton County.

The defense was headed by the formidable Eph Inman, one of the best-known criminal lawyers in Indiana, assisted by Floyd Christian, an experienced trial lawyer from Noblesville, and Ira Holmes, a lawyer from Indianapolis equally experienced in both civil and criminal cases.

Cox made the opening statement to the jury of what the state intended to prove. The defense waived its right to reply, and the prosecution began presenting the first of its twenty-eight witnesses.

The basic chain of events was soon on record: Madge's walk to Stephenson's house with Gentry, the train trip to Hammond, the telegram to her mother, and the return of Madge to her home by Klinck. Dr. Kingsbury, Madge's parents, and a nurse who attended her testified as to Madge's condition when she was returned home. She was in a state of shock, had a rapid pulse, her body was blue and cold, and there were lacerations and bruises on her face, mouth, and breasts.

Over strenuous defense objections, Madge's dying declaration was admitted in evidence, with only a few minor deletions. Several witnesses—the Pullman porter and conductor who had seen Madge, Stephenson, and Gentry on the train; the hotel clerk and a porter who had seen them at the Indiana Hotel in Hammond; the hotel maid who had seen bloodstains on the pillow slip in the hotel room and a cuspidor filled with what looked like sour milk—were called to corroborate it wherever possible. Inman's cross-examination produced only minor discrepancies.

From there on the bulk of the state's case was based on the testimony of medical specialists. The goal, it soon became clear, was to prove the third count of the murder indictment: that Madge Oberholtzer's death was not solely the result of self-administered poison, but that it was caused by the complications of a secondary infection resulting from a bite inflicted by Stephenson; that indeed she had shown signs of recovery from the poison when the infection began to take its toll.

A major medical witness, along with Madge's family doctor, Kingsbury, was Dr. Virgil Moon, chairman of the pathology department at the Indiana University School of Medicine, who had done the autopsy on Madge. Dr. Moon said she had suffered acute nephritis, a severe irritation of the intestinal tract and degeneration of heart and liver tissue—all, in his opinion, the result of the bichloride of mercury she had taken. But he also said that among the lacerations on her body, which had healed, one on a breast had suppurated before it healed over; that he had found an abscess in the outer part of the lung below it. This abscess contained pus and staphylococci germs. Some of the same bacteria were found in the kidneys. The effects of the poison on her kidneys had run its course, he said, and new tissue was replacing the damaged tissue. But blood and urine samples showed a secondary infection in ureter tubes and bladder. This, along with the nephritis, caused her death, in his opinion.

An experienced biochemist, Dr. R. N. Harger, testified in detail as to the effects of bichloride of mercury on the human body. All of the state's medical witnesses agreed that the twenty-four-hour delay in getting proper treatment for Madge to eliminate the poison had lessened her chances for recovery.

Finally, in a long question summarizing their testimony,

151

Cox asked three of the medical experts directly to state their opinion of the cause of Madge's death. All three said they believed death came from a complication of a secondary bloodstream infection, with pus-forming bacteria superimposed on the nephritis caused by the bichloride of mercury. Also, they said the infection had probably been caused by a human bite on the woman's breast. Because Madge lived for twenty-nine days after taking the poison, they said, and because the restorative process in the kidneys was well underway, she probably would have recovered except for the secondary infection caused by the bite. (Penicillin was still unknown.)

For the defense, Eph Inman cross-examined each medical witness. Among other things, he tried to draw out accepted facts about bichloride of mercury, which he would use later with his own witnesses. If the poison were taken on an empty stomach, would the effects be quicker? Answer, yes. (Madge had had only coffee for breakfast.) If vomiting occurred would this help? Again, yes. Was milk a proper agent to induce vomiting? Yes. (Stephenson had given milk to Madge in the hotel.)

Inman then set out to try to prove that the poison alone, not the bite, had caused death. His chief defense witness was an Indianapolis physician who professed wide experience in bichloride of mercury cases. He supported the statements drawn by Inman from the state witnesses: the empty stomach, the milk, the vomiting. He added that bichloride of mercury is readily absorbed from any bodily surface. He said that if the poison expelled by vomiting struck the breast, abdomen, or another bodily surface and remained there for some time, it could inflame and corrode those surfaces. He said he knew of cases where frequent use of bichloride of mercury in vaginal douches had caused death.

Madge's father had said that a few months before she died she had had an attack of influenza. Inman's witness said that all kinds of problems could follow a flu attack. If a patient had an abscess on a lung infected with staphylococci, there was no way of determining where it came from. It could have resulted from a previous flu.

Inman could not deny that Madge had wounds on her body, but he insisted that all, including the one that suppurated, had healed. Then he asked the witness directly what, in his opinion, caused Madge's death. The witness said only bichloride of mercury. He added that after a six-hour delay in vomiting up the poison—the length of time Madge had concealed her poisoning from Stephenson—no follow-up treatment could have saved her life. Six other medical witnesses for the defense—all physicians—also said they believed that the bichloride of mercury itself was the cause of Madge's death.

Charles Cox's cross-examination of the chief defense medical witness was a masterpiece of careful advance preparation. He drew out the fact that of the twenty patients the doctor had treated for bichloride of mercury poisoning, all but two or three had died; that the witness had never actually seen the autopsy findings; that one of the main texts he had cited for his reading in toxicology had been written for veterinarians; that the doctor had once taught toxicology, but in a college for veterinarians. Stephenson himself, it was brought out, had been among the doctor's patients. He had prescribed for Stephenson two or three times for alcoholism.

During the entire trial, neither Stephenson, nor Gentry, nor Klinck took the witness stand in his own defense. Klinck, it was established, had not been present on the train trip or in the Hammond Hotel. He had stayed in Indianapolis, and the record showed he was on duty in his capacity as a deputy sheriff in Marion County at the time of the trip. He had been charged as a result of his participation in Madge's alleged abduction from Stephenson's house. Stephenson's chauffeur, Shorty (real name De-Friese), who might have been called by either side, had fled the jurisdiction and was nowhere to be found.

(Meanwhile, ironically, in the midst of the trial, on November 3, the candidate Stephenson had picked for mayor of Indianapolis the preceding spring, John Duvall, was swept to victory in the 1925 municipal elections, along with several of Stephenson's choices for the city council.)

Whether Madge had been forcibly abducted on the night of March 15, as charged in the first count of the indictment, became another, but not a difficult, issue. The defense called a series of witnesses in an effort to show that Madge's relations with Stephenson before that night had been much more intimate than had been indicated, that her trip to Hammond with Stephenson had quite probably been voluntary, and that there had been no need to forcibly ravish her.

Twelve witnesses were called to testify that they had seen Madge and Stephenson together in his office; that they had seen them drinking liquor together; that they had heard Madge call Stephenson "Stevie" and "dear." All of the witnesses, as it turned out, were close friends of Stephenson, most of them associated with him in Klan activities.

The idea that Madge had gone voluntarily to the train with Stephenson was soon put to rest by the state's Ralph Kane during the final arguments. Madge had gone to Stephenson's house with only the clothes she was wearing. Kane said, "If Madge Oberholtzer had gone willingly with Stephenson that night, she would have done it by pre-arrangement, and she would have worn a hat. If I understand anything about women, when they start on a 250-mile [round-trip, Indianapolis-Chicago] Pullman ride they take along their clothes, their hats, their cosmetics, their lingerie."

Also, Kane said, if Madge had intended to be intimate with Stephenson, "do you think she would ever have had that big, pug-nosed Gentry in the same compartment?" He continued, "If she was a willing companion, why bring her home looking like she had been in a fight?" He again read the testimony of the nurse as to Madge's condition, then said sarcastically, "A willing victim, eh? Oh gentlemen, she

The Stephenson mansion, a former sorority house, in the Indianapolis suburb of Irvington. The pillared front was added by Stephenson. From here, Madge Oberholtzer was abducted for her fatal train trip.

D. C. Stephenson, looking ready for a night on the town. (*Louisville Courier-Journal*)

Madge Oberholtzer, not long before she was kidnapped, raped, and mutilated by Stephenson. Her dying declaration, signed and witnessed, sent the would-be Emperor to prison for murder.

D. C. Stephenson, having served thirty years for second degree murder, leaves a hotel room in Michigan City, Indiana, 22 December 1956. His earlier threats, pleas, and appeals could not gain him clemency, for the Klan had effectively fallen apart with his conviction. (A.P./Wide World Photos)

Hic Jacit. Stephenson's tombstone in the Veterans Administration cemetery near Jonesboro, Tennessee. (*Louisville Courier-Journal*)

wasn't hurt. Oh no, she just went along with Stephenson because she loved him."

Bites, germs, and infection aside, the state still wanted to establish the second and fourth counts of the indictment: that the defendants had by their actions put Madge in such a state of pain and mental distraction that she was driven to take poison, and that they thereby were guilty of murder. Ralph Kane presented this argument:

The theory of the law, maintained by the State in this case, has been the law of England for more than 500 years, and it was the law of this country ever since the English common law was brought to this country. I don't care anything about germs. When these defendants unlawfully abducted Madge Oberholtzer, attacked her and dragged her to Hammond, they made themselves criminals, and by that very act drove that poor girl, honored and respected in her community, loved by all, drove her into a position where she lost all, where she was bereft of all she cherished, and forced her to take the poison of death. By those acts D. C. Stephenson and his cohorts became murderers just the same as if they had plunged a dagger into her throbbing heart.

(Later, during an unsuccessful appeal of the case, the Indiana Supreme Court would support Kane's argument by saying, among other things: "When a suicide follows a wound inflicted by a defendant, his act is homicidal, if deceased was rendered irresponsible by the wound and as a natural result of it.")

Kane's statements came as part of a final summation to the jury, for which each side was given a maximum of eight hours. The meticulous Remy had opened the summation for the state with a carefully prepared résumé of the state's evidence. In summary, he said, "Madge Oberholtzer is dead. She would be alive today were it not the unlawful act of these three men. They have destroyed her body, they tried to destroy her soul, and in the last few days they have tried to dishonor her character." He waved a copy of Madge's dying declaration. "Madge Oberholtzer's story still stands untarnished. Her dying declaration is before you again with corroborating evidence from witness after witness, credible witnesses. It stands not only with the solemnity of a person who faces certain death, it still stands after all the evidence is in, most of it not even denied."

Inman began his final argument to the jury by stating the indictment of Stephenson, Gentry, and Klinck was the result of hostility toward Stephenson: "I sincerely believe that such an indictment would not have been returned except that the state's attorney and those privately employed to reap the vengeance of hate [were] determined to respond to the wishes of the unreasoning element of hostility which aims to bring Stephenson to destruction."

Inman then concentrated on his main hope for acquittal. He said: "The sole question presented here is: Can suicide be murder? Can suicide be homicide?" He denounced Madge's "so-called dying declaration" as a "lawyer-made declaration designed as poisonous propaganda to be used in an effort to gain money." If it declared anything, he said,

> It is a dying declaration of suicide and not homicide. She, by her own concealment of taking the poison for six hours, made medical aid of no avail. She, by her own willful act of conduct, made it impossible for these men to save her life. The dying declaration was made by the girl for the justification of herself, to free herself from fault and place the blame on others, to put her right with her family and friends.

The case went to the jury a little before noon on Saturday, November 14. In his instructions to the jury, Judge Sparks had explained that, with a guilty finding, they had three choices: First-degree murder, which the state asked, had a death or life sentence. First degree murder would require a finding that the accused had acted with premeditation, with purposeful intent to kill, or in the perpetration of or intent to rape, commit arson, robbery, or burglary. Then there was second-degree murder, the killing of a person maliciously but without premeditation. This could bring a maximum life sentence. Finally, there was manslaughter, a killing committed in the heat of anger, or suddenly and involuntarily, without actual malice, with sentences varying in numbers of years.

The jury was out about six hours. It found Stephenson guilty of second-degree murder and said he should be imprisoned for life. Gentry and Klinck were acquitted, but they were not out of the hands of the law. Both were returned to Indianapolis under a five-thousand-dollar bond to face charges of arson in the April fire at Stephenson's Irvington mansion.[1]

The court's judgment on the Stephenson verdict came on Monday, November 16. Just before he passed the life sentence, Judge Sparks asked Stephenson, "Has the prisoner anything to say before my sentence is pronounced." Stephenson, who had been calmly chewing an unlighted cigar, stepped forward:

> I have this to say. I am not guilty of this charge of murder or any lesser degree of homicide. It has always been my understanding that no man could be deprived of his liberty without due process of law. I believe the opinion is universal that from the surrounding circumstances of this trial the procedure was not by due process of law.
>
> About three hundred and fifty people sat in this courtroom out of three and a half million in the State of Indiana, and applauded the things said against me and hissed the pleas in my behalf. In this situation the jury had no way of arriving calmly and impartially at a verdict.
>
> Time will unfold the cold white light of truth and show this honorable court and the world that D. C. Stephenson is not guilty of this or any other charge brought against him.[2]

One of Stephenson's defense attorneys, Floyd Christian, said that he had been "hissed repeatedly" by courtroom spectators during his final argument. The judge said he had not heard hissing. "My hearing is not of the best," he said, "and I never heard any hissing if it occurred. I am very sorry." The judge also said he hoped what Stephenson said about his innocence was true and that, "if it is true that he is innocent, time will tell and it ought to tell."[3]

Shortly after the sentence was passed, Stephenson called reporters to his jail cell and issued a long, rambling statement again denying his guilt and calling his conviction the result of pressures by his enemies:

> In the atmosphere which surrounded the entire proceedings, a fair and impartial trial was impossible. Carefully shielded but powerful influences which converted money into malicious stories and evil propaganda had done their work by influencing a certain element of people to a point where they gave expression in the form of signed resolutions and demonstrations in the courtroom which have heretofore been unheard of in a civilized country, excepting alone perhaps Russia. . . . The very nature of the whole proceedings brands it as the most appalling persecution to which man has been subjected since the days when civilization abandoned the bludgeon and accepted due process of law. . . . The tide of hate so started only goes so far; then it must return; it will return.
>
> I am not guilty of murder or lesser included degrees of homicide, nor of the other charges or allegations made by the combined forces that were arrayed against me, and when time turns the cold white light of truth upon the present black cloud of falsehood the public will shudder with consternation.

He paid tribute to the "eminent gentlemen" who had been his defense lawyers and said "they will fight on . . . to final victory" until this "outrage upon justice . . . has been rectified and I obtain my liberty. . . . I do not intend to be a sacrificial lamb that will be offered up as the political scapegoat for the whole state of Indiana."[4] Reporters who later found him lying on his back in his cell quoted him as saying, "Surrender? I'm just beginning to fight. The last chapter has not been written."

Five days later, on the morning of November 21, the once-powerful Grand Dragon who had said he was "the law" entered Indiana State Prison in Michigan City as prisoner 11148. He was thirty-four years old. He would be sixty-five before he finally went free.

10

The "Black Boxes"

THE D. C. STEPHENSON SCANDAL killed the Ku Klux Klan in Indiana. Soon the death knell would be spreading across the Klan's other northern realms as well. As Norman Weaver observed, "If Stephenson had been convicted of robbery, or graft, of corrupt practices in political affairs, the Klan might have survived." But the "repulsive character" of the case drove Klansmen out of the Invisible Empire in throngs.[1]

In 1924 the Indiana Klan had an estimated membership of at least a quarter-million—possibly 300,000. Within a year after Stephenson's conviction, it had dropped to only a few thousand. Pastors who had once extolled the Klan as a force for God and country now fell silent and tried to forget what they had said. Merchants who had once displayed "TWK" (trade with a Klansman) signs now hurried to destroy them. Most important, the politicians who had once courted Klan support now began a hasty exodus. "For years to come," wrote John Bartlow Martin, " 'Stephensonism' would be a label fatal to any Indiana politician. They all knew it; they scurried for cover."[2]

The fact that there was "another Klan" opposed to Stephenson long before his arrest seems to have been forgotten, or overlooked. Stephenson had in fact been banished from the national Klan wing for "gross immorality" even before he met Madge Oberholtzer.

Some Klansmen tried to keep their organization viable by publicly divorcing themselves from him. Among several efforts of anti-Stephenson Klansmen to shed the Stephenson image was a letter from the Elkhart County Klan to the judge and jury and all attorneys involved in his conviction. The letter, released to newspapers, read: "We the Klansmen of Elkhart County Klan No. 77, Realm of Indiana, wish to express our gratitude and sincere appreciation for the conviction and manner in which you conducted the trial of one David C. Stephenson. May each of you ever stand true to the law of our land against any individual or group of individuals who try to violate American laws and principles." Despite such efforts, the public was in no mood to sort all this out. The Klan was Stephenson and now something to be shunned.

All that was left, said Weaver,

> were a few fanatical groups in some of the cities and towns that tried to revive the Klan on the issue of public schools, and the regular Klan leaders who remained to fight over the spoils. . . . By the time of the 1927 legislature the Klan was a forgotten issue. One rugged individual, a hold-over from the 1925 session, introduced a bill to make all teachers in the state be graduates of the public schools [but] other members, mockingly, reminded him that those days were over. By 1927 the Klan had died out to all extents and purposes.[3]

As late as 1944, when Robert W. Lyons, a millionaire chain store lobbyist, was elected Republican national committeeman, one of his Republican opponents accused him of former connections and intrigues with the Klan. Lyons quickly resigned.

As he headed for the state prison through the dawn on November 21, 1925, it is doubtful if D. C. Stephenson thought all of this through. His conviction, he would insist,

had been a miscarriage of justice engineered by his enemies. Whatever else he had done, he was not guilty of
murder. There would be appeals to higher courts. Most
important of all, he was hopeful he would soon win a pardon
or a parole from the man who owed him so much, Indiana's
governor, Ed Jackson.

As the months went by, however, there was only silence
from the governor's office. Jackson too had scurried for cover
from both Stephenson and the Klan. Then, by early 1926,
reports began leaking out from the prison that Stephenson
was preparing to divulge information that would link many
high-ranking Indiana politicians in deals and corruption
involving the Klan. The reports, of course, originated with
Stephenson himself. They were obviously part of a calculated plan to bring pressure on Jackson for clemency before
he himself was exposed, and also to lead other fearful
politicians to bring pressure on Jackson in order to protect
themselves.

Stephenson was well prepared. One attorney, Floyd
Christian, would later tell a grand jury that he had seen
Stephenson in his jail cell pinning several checks to some
papers. Christian asked him what he was doing, he recalled, and Stephenson said, "I am getting my ammunition
ready."

"Steve then showed me some of the letters and checks
which were piled upon the bunk in that cell," Christian
said. "I have no idea as to the number of them, except that
the bunk which they were on was about 6½ feet long by 3½
feet wide [and] was stacked with checks and papers, some
of which I examined in a casual manner." Christian said
he saw among these documents at least two checks made
out to Jackson, including one, as he recalled, for five-
thousand-dollars.[4]

For Stephenson, getting reports and rumors out of the
prison was not difficult. Throughout much of 1926 he had
ready access to many visitors, in addition to his attorneys.
When more time passed without action, he decided to go
public—but only a step at a time, still leaving leeway for

161

Jackson to act. Through one of his visitors, Court Asher, the Muncie bootlegger and former Klan associate, a long letter and a facsimile of Stephenson's contract with Indianapolis's Klansman mayor, John Duvall, were smuggled out of prison. The facsimile was a copy of the written pledge of Duvall promising Stephenson control of appointments to the city's board of public works, park board, and safety board, which controlled the police department. Asher made the documents available to Boyd Gurley, editor of the *Indianapolis Times*. Soon the *Times* would be in hot pursuit of other details.

Another Stephenson visitor—a man of far higher reputation and integrity—was Thomas H. Adams, editor and publisher of the *Vincennes Commercial*. As he had to Asher, Stephenson told Adams of two metal black boxes, hidden somewhere in Indiana, which he said concealed checks and records documenting many shady dealings with politicians. Adams was a lifelong Republican and an active member of the Indiana Republican Editorial Association. He knew his party might suffer, but as a responsible editor and citizen he felt the matter should be cleared up publicly. Other Republicans pressured him to let sleeping dogs lie. Finally, however, Adams took the lead in organizing a meeting of fifteen prominent Indiana editors where Jackson was invited to appear and defend himself. Jackson promised to attend but never showed up.

Adams continued to press publicly for an investigation. On October 8, 1926, at a Republican rally in LaGrange, Indiana, Jackson replied with a promise of a thorough investigation into Stephenson's charges. In a speech that may have set a high for political deviousness, the man who within a year would himself be indicted for conspiracy and bribery said:

> The people of Indiana are entitled to clean and wholesome government. They are entitled to clean, honest, upright, intelligent public servants and public service. If in any department of the state service it can be shown that graft,

dishonesty, corruption or malfeasance existed, your executive will do his share in its exposure and in the prosecution and punishment of the offenders. . . . The Republican party of the state has always stood for clean government and has always led in the exposure of graft and corruption wherever it may be found, even within its own ranks. . . . Its present leadership pledges its enthusiastic efforts to the punishment [sic] of all offenders against honesty and common decency.[5]

The governor was followed by Theodore Roosevelt, Jr. The *Indianapolis News* reported that "Roosevelt also referred to the Indiana accusations of political corruption and expressed himself as satisfied the Republicans of Indiana under leadership of the Governor will investigate freely and frankly whatever situation may exist and demand proper punishment for any proved guilty."

Only a week later the *Indianapolis Times* began a series of long articles on "What Stephenson Could Tell"—based on the Stephenson letters smuggled from the prison—about graft in public office; about protection money paid by large bootlegging interests; about money Stephenson had raised from public utility groups for the Republican State Committee which wound up in the pocket of "one individual" (later identified as Jackson); about pressures and influence on the courts for favorable decisions; about $200,000 spent in 1924 to "buy votes" and "stuff ballot boxes."[6] The articles were accompanied by large facsimile illustrations of the major letter in Stephenson's own handwriting.

Soon the Marion County prosecutor, William H. Remy, and a special grand jury were pressing an investigation. Both Asher and Adams were among those called to testify. Then, on October 13, 1926, D. C. Stephenson himself was brought from the prison to appear before the grand jury. Remy asked him about the Duvall contract letter, about the black boxes and the checks described by Christian, and about the *Times* articles on "what he could tell."

Stephenson refused to answer. He said he was standing on his constitutional rights against self-incrimination. Quite possibly, however, he thought Governor Jackson

163

would still change his mind and grant him clemency to limit further disclosures. He was mistaken; there was no response from the governor's office.

In May of 1927 Jackson got his last chance. Stephenson asked him for at least a ninety-day parole. Jackson refused. He said, "D. C. Stephenson is guilty of the murder of a young girl, and I will not be blackmailed into giving him a pardon." Stephenson then decided to talk. Soon he asked Prosecutor Remy to come to the prison. In a long conference on July 1, he divulged much information about his dealings with Jackson and others. He also agreed to deliver up the black boxes. Soon he would again be before the grand jury.

Apparently in preparation for this, Stephenson on July 13 publicly released through an attorney facsimiles of thirty-one checks that he said were for Jackson's primary and general election campaigns. The largest was for twenty-five hundred dollars, made out personally to Jackson. Jackson had previously denied receiving any money from Stephenson. When asked about this check, he recalled that it was in payment for a horse named "Senator" that he had sold to Stephenson. When the horse couldn't be found, investigators were told it had "choked to death on a corn cob."

The black boxes—two metal containers about eighteen inches long, eight inches wide and eight inches deep—were hidden in a barn on a farm near the little town of Lick Skillet in southwestern Indiana, about eight miles south of Washington. Deputy prosecutors from Marion County went there for a prearranged meeting with Stephenson's former coal business partner, Julian, who delivered up the boxes and keys.

The boxes were not quite the treasure trove expected, but they did contain copies of thirty-one checks with Stephenson's notations as to their recipients and usually their purposes. Some were to Jackson himself, others to his supporters. The boxes also contained written pledges from a congressman from Indianapolis, Ralph Updike, and another from Congressman Harry Rowbottom, of Evansville, promising to let Stephenson dictate their patronage appointments in return for his support in the election.

In addition to the boxes, prosecutors recovered stacks of letters to Stephenson and carbon copies of his replies—enough, the *Times* reported, "to fill the back end of an automobile." Many were of little value. There were letters to Stephenson from assorted nonpolitical people seeking loans, which were refused. Many were moldy at the bottom and appeared to have been buried for many months.

Stephenson was brought before a new Marion County grand jury on July 31, 1927. (The previous grand jury had been discharged after reports of attempted bribery.) He was now a willing witness. He talked freely about the checks. The largest was one for twenty-five hundred dollars dated September 12, 1923, and made out personally to Jackson, then Indiana secretary of state. Stephenson said it was the first part of ten-thousand-dollars given to Jackson for his primary election campaign for governor in late 1923 and early 1924. He said the check was given to Jackson "sitting on my back porch at 5432 University Avenue." (The ten-thousand-dollar figure included only money given personally to Jackson. Later Stephenson would say he spent more than seventy-three-thousand-dollars on Jackson's primary campaign, even more on the general election.)

Another five-thousand-dollars, he said, was paid in cash to Jackson at his home on December 24, 1923. Stephenson told the grand jury that upon the December cash payment, Jackson "gave me a second-hand Marlin shotgun that night for a Christmas present. I don't know whether he considers I bought a second-hand shotgun for $5,000 or not." The remaining twenty-five hundred dollars for the primary election campaign was delivered in cash to Jackson in his secretary of state's office in Indianapolis. Asked if, to his knowledge, these campaign contributions were reported, Stephenson said, "No! I knew he was not going to report it."

Stephenson said Jackson collected even more through a misappropriation of funds contributed by public utilities to the Republican State Committee in 1924. He told how he had raised some twenty-three-thousand-dollars from utility interests for the Republican State Committee to aid the Republican party in the 1924 election. This, he said, included about fifteen-thousand-dollars from the Insull Utility Group in Chicago, which had interests in Indiana, and other money from the telephone company and water company in Indianapolis. The money was given to Jackson personally to turn over to the Republican State Committee. But, Stephenson said, "he never delivered a dime of it to the Committee. He bought a farm over in Hancock County with part of it, paid off a note, and stuck the rest in his sock."

Stephenson also told of other checks to W. H. ("Big Jack") Jackson, the black Republican publisher of a newspaper widely read in the Indianapolis black community, for "publicity for Ed," and to a black preacher, the Reverend C. T. Sanders, for helping in Jackson's campaign.

All in all, he told the jury, he spent about $227,000 for Jackson's primary and general election campaigns. But it was not charity. Stephenson said, "I had a written contract with him that I was to get it back by getting the coal contract from the State, by control of the Highway Commission, and of the State Purchasing Department." He also told of the pledge from Mayor Duvall of Indianapolis, promising him control of the city's board of public works, park board and safety board.

The most damaging testimony against Jackson, however, involved the attempted bribery of Governor Warren McCray in 1923. Jackson was then Indiana secretary of state. Stephenson told how Jackson, as an agent of the Klan, had approached McCray with $10,000 on December 8, 1923. McCray could have it if he would appoint a Klan attorney, James E. McDonald, to fill a vacancy as Marion County prosecutor. (McCray had refused, and appointed William Remy instead.) As a result of this testimony, Governor Jackson was indicted on September 9, 1927, for conspiracy and bribery, along with George V. (Cap) Coffin, the Marion

County Klansman Republican chairman, and Robert Marsh, a Klan attorney. Stephenson was included in the indictment but was never tried, having turned state's evidence. After several legal maneuvers, Jackson, Coffin, and Marsh would come to trial in February 1928.

Meanwhile, through the summer and fall of 1926, the *Indianapolis Times,* Remy, and the grand jury had also been pursuing reports of political corruption involving Indianapolis's Klansman Mayor John Duvall, the Klan-dominated city council, and other minor city officials. It was a tangled web, including the Klan, a slot machine boss, and even the pastor of a Methodist church.

Duvall's letter promising Stephenson control of several city boards and the police department was already on record, but he had also made promises to others. It was charged that Duvall had accepted a fourteen-thousand-dollar contribution to his 1925 campaign from William H. ("Big Bill") Armitage, reputed Marion County slot machine king, in return for promises similar to those made to Stephenson: control of various city boards and agencies. More to the point, he had failed to report this contribution, in violation of the Indiana Corrupt Practices Act.

At the Klan-church level, Duvall had also promised the Reverend George Henninger, pastor of the East Tenth Street Methodist Church and head of the Ku Klux Klan Political Action Committee, that he would make 85 percent of his appointments from persons recommended by the Klan, and that he would appoint no Catholics. George S. Elliott, an Indianapolis attorney and Exalted Cyclops of the Indianapolis Klan, was promised the job of city purchasing agent. (By the time of the Indianapolis mayoral campaign in November 1925, Stephenson was on trial for murder in Noblesville. Duvall's promises to him and others had been made in the early spring, considerably before the scandal broke.)

Duvall was indicted for violating the State Corrupt Practices Act. Six Republican Klansmen of the city council were also indicted for soliciting or accepting bribes. One typical example of the numerous petty shakedowns was described by an Indianapolis resident who had come to the city council to get a minor zoning variance. When he was refused, someone told him privately to "see Boynton Moore. . . . He will fix you up." Moore, a Klansman, was president of the city council.

When he went to see Moore, he testified, Moore said,

"Sure, we can do it for you. You citizens deserve a break." I thanked him and started to walk away and he says, "No, just a minute, there will be a little expense to this thing and you'll have to put up $100.00 to take care of the boys' expenses." I told him I wasn't interested. Moore then offered to have it done for $50.00, then $25.00, finally for $10. . . . I gave him $10 and my variance went through.[7]

Other minor city officials were also charged with soliciting bribes, even including one who got a five-dollar pay-off from an applicant for a market stall. Moore was later also indicted on a charge of taking a one-hundred-dollar bribe not to vote for impeachment of Duvall by the city council. He was found guilty, but was pardoned by Jackson.

Duvall went on trial on September 12, 1927, on charges of violating the Indiana Corrupt Practices Act. He was convicted, fined one-thousand-dollars, and sentenced to thirty days in jail. The court also ruled that he was barred from holding public office, retroactive to January 1, 1926. He resigned next month, and the council replaced him with Ert Slack, a Democratic lawyer. After a lengthy appeal, Duvall finally served his jail term. The six Klan city council members and other minor officials pleaded guilty to lesser charges of corruption, paid small fines, and resigned.

On February 9, 1928, Governor Jackson, George V. "Cap" Coffin, the Marion County Klansman Republican boss, and Klan lawyer Robert I. Marsh, went on trial in the Marion County Circuit Court. The indictment against them charged:

On or about December 8, 1923 . . . one Ed Jackson, then Secretary of State, and one Robert I. Marsh and one George

V. Coffin did then and there feloniously and unlawfully unite, conspire, confederate and agree with each other and with one David C. Stephenson to feloniously bribe and offer to bribe one Warren T. McCray, then Governor of Indiana, by offering him $10,000 in lawful United States currency to appoint one James E. McDonald as Prosecuting Attorney of Marion County to fill a vacancy, said appointment being the official duty of such Governor. . . . And your [grand] jurors further allege that the defendants concealed such crime.

(Though named in the indictment, Stephenson was not put on trial—a reward for having turned state's evidence.)

The charge of concealment was crucial. If there had been active concealment, the two-year statute of limitations would not apply. It had been nearly four years between the time of the alleged bribe and the time the first charges were brought.

Among witnesses for Remy were Stephenson and former governor McCray, then on parole from the federal penitentiary in Atlanta, where he had been sent for using the mails to defraud in an embezzlement of state funds. Through these witnesses and others, the facts of the bribe attempt were soon established. McCray described how he turned down the ten-thousand-dollar offer—even at a time when he was facing trial for fraudulent misuse of state funds and was promised other help to avoid a conviction. He said he told Jackson, "It looks like I have lost my fortune [a multimillion dollar cattle business] . . . and my office is threatened, and my liberty, but I am not going to surrender my self-respect."

That Jackson, Coffin, and Marsh were guilty was clearly established, but all three men went free under the two-year statute of limitations. It had been well over three-and-a-half years between the time of the bribe and the time charges were brought. The crucial question was: Did they actively try to conceal their crime? Judge Charles McCabe found that they were not proved to have done so. He told the jury:

Although the State has proved a conspiracy by all the defendants that the bribe took place, it was not proved a positive act of concealment. Under Indiana law, if a felony charge is not filed within two years of the act, homicide excepted, the defendant cannot be convicted unless he has been out of the state or concealed the crime. Therefore, I instruct you to return a verdict in this case of "Not Guilty" as to all defendants.

Jackson was pressured to resign, but he returned to the statehouse and finished his term. Coffin, however, managed to keep control of the Republican apparatus in Marion County while Marsh returned to his law practice.

For its part in exposing much of the Klan-connected corruption the *Times* was awarded the Pulitzer Prize for Meritorious Public Service in 1928. The stalwart and incorruptible prosecutor, William H. Remy, would long be remembered for his dogged pursuit of Klan-connected crime and would go on to many more years of faithful public service. D. C. Stephenson, the once-powerful Grand Dragon, would go back to many more years of confinement in the Indiana State Prison.

11

Appeals: "Hope Springs Eternal . . ."

BACK BEHIND THE WALLS of the Indiana State Prison at Michigan City, D. C. Stephenson pursued his long fight for freedom. For years he continued to insist that he had been "framed" by a group of Indiana politicians working with his enemies in the Evans-Bossert wing of the Ku Klux Klan.

Through a long succession of attorneys, he continued to appeal to the courts, both state and federal. From the late 1920s through the early 1940s, some forty separate legal actions were filed seeking to void or ameliorate his murder sentence. There were appeals for a new trial, for writs of *error coram nobis,* for writs of habeas corpus, for changes of judges, for temporary bail . . .

Petitions for *error coram nobis,* an ancient common law writ to compel the setting aside of a verdict, were filed in both the Hamilton County Circuit Court and the Indiana Supreme Court. Among other things, it was claimed that Imperial Wizard Evans and his allies had used Madge Oberholtzer to trap Stephenson; that the attorney who prepared Madge's dying declaration, Asa J. Smith, was part of a Klan conspiracy against him; that he had not been able to take the witness stand to give proof of these things because of threats on his life.

One can only speculate whether Stephenson himself really believed all of this. His record showed he had a higher than average capacity for self-delusion. Later, in connection with one of his many appeals to the parole board, a psychiatrist who examined him reported that Stephenson was suffering from paranoia. In any event, few others believed him. To the vast majority of people, as well as to the courts, his abduction of Madge Oberholtzer and his sadistic assault of her had been proved in a fair trial before an impartial judge and jury.

But had he also been proved guilty of murder?

This question, wrote Francis X. Busch in a detailed and objective analysis of several notable American trials, including those of Samuel Insull and Alger Hiss,

> is not so easily disposed of. Out of the maze of legal charges and denials the jury found that Stephenson drugged the girl and then forced her against her will to accompany him to the train and into the drawing room; that he not only criminally assaulted her but subjected her to almost unbelievably cruel and inhumane treatment; that as a direct consequence of his criminal acts she became deranged to the point that she took the poison which ended her life.[1]

Medical experts had testified that an infection resulting from a wound inflicted by Stephenson had been one cause of Madge Oberholtzer's death. But they also said the wound was aggravated by the poison, a combination that proved fatal. Without the poison, would the wound alone have caused death? Stephenson's attorneys said no. But did not Stephenson's attack drive her to take poison, and did not this make the attacker guilty of murder? Stephenson's lawyers said it did not. After the attack, they pointed out, she was able to leave the train and walk a block to a hotel in Hammond, have coffee, worry that she had no hat, and go with Stephenson's chauffeur to buy one.

"It is further arguable," Busch wrote,

that from the time she left the train she was a free agent and could at any time have summoned help or escaped from Stephenson and his agents; that she took the poison without his knowledge and outside of his presence; and that, in summary, her actions subsequent to the assault and before the taking of the poison showed a complete absence of fear of further bodily harm, irrationality or hysteria, and therefore the essential "causal connection" between the assault and the suicide was lacking.[2]

This contention was, among others, presented by Stephenson's lawyers in an appeal to the Indiana Supreme Court. A majority rejected it. "When suicide follows a wound inflicted by a defendant" the opinion stated, "his act is homicidal, if deceased was rendered irresponsible by the wound and as the natural result of it."

"We should think," the court added, "the same rule would apply if a defendant engaged in the commission of a felony such as rape or attempted rape . . . inflicts upon his victim both physical and mental injuries the natural and probable result of which would render the deceased mentally irresponsible and suicide followed."

The court noted Madge Oberholtzer's uncontested assertion that at one time she considered taking Stephenson's revolver and shooting herself. "The same forces," the court said, "the same impulses that would impel her to shoot herself were pressing and overwhelming her at the time she swallowed the poison. . . . To say that there is no causal connection between the acts of appellant and the death of Madge Oberholtzer, and that the treatment accorded her by appellant had no causal connection with the death of Madge Oberholtzer would be a travesty of justice."

In its conclusion the court stated, "The evidence was sufficient and justified the jury in finding that appellant by his acts and conduct rendered the deceased distracted and mentally irresponsible, and that such was the natural and probable consequence of willful and criminal treatment, and that the appellant was guilty of murder in the second degree."[3]

Most people seemed satisfied with the court's ruling. However, some, Stephenson's friends as well as more objective observers, questioned the attack-suicide link. Stephenson himself once wrote to an Indiana reporter, "I should have been put in jail for my political activities, but I am not guilty of murder."

In 1939, through an Indianapolis newspaper reporter, Stephenson engineered a book still trying to prove that he had been framed. It began with a letter to Robert A. Butler, a former *Indianapolis News* reporter, dated October 24, 1939. It was written in the Noblesville jail, where Stephenson was held during an appeal to the Hamilton County Circuit Court.

> Information has come to me through one of our mutual friends that you are now a free-lance writer, and not connected with any particular newspaper. Assuming this is a fact, I have a very unusual and important request to make.
>
> You know, as all Indiana newspapermen know, that I have contended for fourteen years that I was framed by a group of Indiana politicians, working with and through the national headquarters of the klan. . . . I have not changed this contention, and I shall never change. . . . The request I have to make is that you take over the job of thoroughly investigating every feature and ramification of this case, with the purpose of bringing in the facts as you find them. . . . No one connected with my affairs, or speaking with my authority, will disturb you in this investigation, and they will not attempt to guide or influence your work.[4]

The result was a book by Butler called *So They Framed Stephenson*. In it Stephenson described his differences with the national Klan hierarchy and Imperial Wizard Evans. He says he "resigned from the klan because of repeated disagreements with Dr. Evans over national policy of the klan, and because of the character of the men with whom Evans had surrounded himself."

"It was the policy of Evans," he said, "to use women in destroying the reputation of men who opposed him. Edward

Clark Young, Captain William Coburn, and a number of other men had been framed with Mann Act violations when they were wholly innocent of the charges. I protested to Evans against this policy and he replied, 'When you want to get a man, just hang a woman on him.' "[5]

He accused Evans of having a "mania for stirring up hate in the klan against racial and religious groups who were not members of the klan." When Stephenson protested, he said Evans replied, "You gotta give 'em something to hate to keep 'em stirred up."

Stephenson then describes what he says were repeated efforts of Evans and his allies to "hang a woman" on him. They sent "immoral women" to try to get admission to his Irvington home. Another woman, he said, followed him to Chicago on a train and tried to entice him, then followed him back to Indianapolis and registered in a room adjoining his downtown suite at the Washington Hotel. He said she "admitted she was employed by Dr. Hiram Wesley Evans to involve me in a scandal."[6]

He claimed that Asa J. Smith, the lawyer who prepared and took Madge Oberholtzer's "dying declaration" was a Klan lawyer for an opposing faction; that he was not arrested until Smith "came to my office in the Kresge building and demanded one hundred thousand dollars and all of the political papers in my possession." He said Smith "specifically stated" that the political papers included Klan slates for the 1924 elections.[7]

Stephenson said he had been on the train to Hammond the early morning of March 16, 1925, but not with Madge Oberholtzer. He was with another woman of similar appearance, the wife of a friend who was having problems that he was trying to help solve. He refused to reveal her name in order to protect her.[8] He further said he had not been able to testify in his own defense at his murder trial because of threats on his life. To support these claims, Butler published affidavits from several people involved in the case, including the Hamilton County sheriff and one of Stephenson's attorneys.

At the close of his affidavit describing the threatening atmosphere created by Klansmen around the Noblesville jail, Sheriff Charles Gooding said that he believed "a grave injustice was done David C. Stephenson when he was tried under circumstances where his defense was completely suppressed by threats against his life and by a well-grounded fear that he would be assassinated if he attempted to testify in his own defense."[9]

In another affidavit, one of Stephenson's defense attorneys, Holmes, said that because of "oral and written threats against the life of the defendant" he had advised Stephenson not to take the witness stand in his own defense. Holmes said it was "obvious" that, if Stephenson tried to testify, "in my opinion, the hostile demonstrations and threats would become action and the defendant would have been killed in the ensuing violence."[10]

The book produced no visible results toward Stephenson's freedom. As the years went on, he appeared repeatedly before the parole board but was turned down each time. Sometimes Madge Oberholtzer's parents, among others, appeared at the hearings to oppose freeing him.

During most of this time, apparently, Stephenson's life in the prison was not difficult or especially unpleasant. In late 1927, he had for a short time been placed in solitary confinement for allegedly smuggling out a letter critical of some statements made by Indiana's senator Arthur Robinson. While other inmates enjoyed Thanksgiving turkey, Stephenson remained in "the hole" on bread and water. The *Indianapolis News* reported that "prison officials said that when [Stephenson] promises to keep quiet about his affairs while in prison he will receive the same privileges that other prisoners have."[11]

This episode, however, was evidently in stark contrast to his regular life in prison. To at least two visitors on one occasion, his lot seemed considerably better than that of most other inmates. Two attorneys who had gone there on other business said they had asked to see the "famous prisoner." As they later told a Marion County deputy prosecutor, the warden said they should send in their cards to him. In a few minutes they were escorted by Stephenson's "Japanese servant" to his private quarters in an isolated part of the prison where he was working as manager of the prison laundry—a promotion from his earlier job in the chair factory.

"They told me later," the deputy prosecutor said, "that Steve was not dressed in prison stripes but wore a natty business suit, white shirt and pearly gray tie, and that he chatted pleasantly with them, asking what was new in Indianapolis."[12]

Finally, on March 23, 1950, after more than twenty-four years in prison, Stephenson won his first parole. It came through a commutation issued by a highly respected Democratic governor with no Klan connections, Henry F. Schricker, but the freedom was short-lived. Stephenson was freed ostensibly to take a job in Carbondale, Illinois. However, he went on to Tulsa, Oklahoma, for a short stay with his daughter, then reportedly to Minneapolis, where he worked as a printer under an alias. Back in Carbondale, he was arrested for failure to report to parole officers and returned to the Indiana prison on December 7, 1951.

In January 1955, he again seemed near freedom. Indiana officials said Stephenson had, reportedly through the sponsorship of a clergyman, been offered a job in Chicago. His parole, however, would be conditioned on the willingness of Illinois to accept him. Illinois parole officials refused, and Stephenson remained a prisoner in Indiana.

At last, a few days before Christmas 1956, Stephenson won a final discharge from Governor George N. Craig. A sister of Stephenson living near Meadville, Pennsylvania, Mrs. Arthur H. Stainbrook, had written prison officials saying, "We will be glad to welcome him and help him forget the past." The Christmas parole was well-timed for the season of peace on earth, good will to men, but it included a less-charitable restriction: Stephenson was to leave Indiana and never return. Hugh O'Brien, chairman of

177

the State Board of Corrections, which recommended clemency, said, "He is free forever unless he comes back to the State of Indiana."[13]

Stephenson did, however, soon come back to Indiana. He returned to Seymour in 1958 and took a third wife, a wealthy widow named Martha Loerz Dickinson, Mrs. Dickinson's late husband, W. F. Dickinson, had been vice-president of a group called Liberty Foundation, Inc., formed in the 1930s to raise funds to help Stephenson win his freedom.

Stephenson lived quietly in Seymour. He socialized little but made no special effort to conceal his presence. Indiana officials were surely aware of his return, but had apparently lost interest in pursuing him. In any event the never-come-back parole provision was of doubtful constitutionality, and there had been no requirement that he report to parole officers.

Meanwhile, Stephenson was busy selling a type-cleaning machine he had invented during his years in prison. He frequently went on sales trips with this equipment, and on one such trip he fell afoul of the law again. In 1961, in Independence, Missouri, at age seventy, he was arrested for assaulting a sixteen-year-old girl, allegedly by trying to force her into his automobile. Stephenson denied the charge and said he had simply stopped to ask the girl directions, when she became frightened.

Despite this defense, the magistrate found him guilty. He was fined three hundred dollars and sentenced to four months in jail. However, the magistrate then released him on condition that he leave the state of Missouri and "never return."

Not long after this episode—perhaps because of it—Stephenson and his third wife separated, though they were not divorced. He left Seymour in 1962 and his wife said she never heard from him again.

D. C. Stephenson died in 1966 in Jonesboro, Tennessee. His final years after leaving Seymour, Indiana, were cloaked in mystery until 1978, when his grave was discovered in a Veterans Administration cemetery near Jonesboro by reporters for the Louisville (Kentucky) *Courier-Journal* after a three-month search.

The search had been sparked by the curiosity and reportorial enterprise of Gordon Englehart, for many years Indianapolis bureau chief of the *Courier-Journal*. In 1977 Englehart had read an *Indianapolis Star* feature story on Stephenson's career that ended with his mysterious disappearance in 1962. Going to work in Louisville later, he began and led a three-month search for Stephenson that extended through Indiana, Oklahoma, Texas, Illinois, Pennsylvania, and Tennessee.

The search finally ended in eastern Tennessee, where Stephenson's grave was found among those of other war veterans in the Mountain Home National Cemetery in Johnson City, near Jonesboro. How and why he had come to Tennessee was not known. But the *Courier-Journal* found he had been admitted in 1963 to the Veterans Administration Mountain Home Hospital and Domiciliary in Johnson City for treatment of a heart condition and filial arthrosis (degeneration of joints). He later went to work for the Jonesboro newspaper, the weekly *Herald & Tribune,* as a printer and part-time writer. At the suggestion of his employers he took an upstairs apartment in the house of a widow, Martha Sutton, a former schoolteacher with deep family roots in Jonesboro.

Meanwhile he continued to market his type-cleaning machine, making frequent trips out of town. During one such lengthy trip to Florida, he and Mrs. Sutton corresponded frequently. When he came back they were married in the Presbyterian Church in Jonesboro on May 26, 1964. He was seventy-two and his wife was fifty-five. Apparently, as Randy Horrell, another renter in Mrs. Sutton's house at the time, later said, "He just swept Mrs. Sutton off her feet." Mrs. Sutton was unaware of his past. There was no evidence of his previous heavy drinking or lechery.

Englehart, in an interview, found the new Mrs. Stephenson a "gracious Southern lady." She said of Stephenson, "I knew nothing of his background, except that I loved him very much and we were married. He was a very wonderful person." They attended church together regularly, she said. Stephenson was especially nice to children, often taking them—both black and white—swimming and buying them ice cream.

On June 28, 1966, Stephenson died, at home in his wife's arms, of a coronary attack. He had expressed a wish to be buried in the Veterans Administration Mountain Home Cemetery rather than in her family plot, his widow said. As she told her story, Englehart wrote, Mrs. Stephenson's eyes misted and she said softly, "I loved him very, very much. My heart was broken when he died. I am sure he is in heaven."[15]

Thus, in June 1966, while angry protestors marched against the Vietnam War and black ghettoes erupted in blazing riots, D. C. Stephenson, about seven weeks' short of his seventy-fifth birthday, was quietly laid to rest among other veterans of the nation's armed forces. Here, in a tree-shaded plot in a Veterans Administration cemetery near a small town in eastern Tennessee, the once-powerful Grand Dragon who dreamed of becoming president is remembered only on a small marble slab with the words:

David C. Stephenson

Texas

2nd Lt. Co. D 36 Infantry

World War I

Aug. 21, 1891   June 28, 1966

Records at the Jonesboro funeral home that handled Stephenson's burial arrangements listed two surviving children: a daughter, Katherine, of Tulsa, Oklahoma, and a son, David James, of Detroit. Neither attended the funeral.

180

Most of Indiana had forgotten him. In Kokomo some remembered the Klan's greatest rally, when tens of thousands had cheered the Grand Dragon at his coronation in Melfalfa Park on the Fourth of July 1923. But the park itself, once a well-kept Klan property, had long been abandoned. As Robert Coughlan wrote in the late 1940s: "The Rev. Everett Nixon carried on for years as secretary of the Melfalfa Park Association, trying to hold together the property and the few believers. But he failed, and now the park is over-grown with brush, deserted and decayed, its sagging pavilion a meeting place for bats and owls."[16]

12

One Klan Dies, Another Rises: The New Klan

THE INVISIBLE EMPIRE never recovered in Middle America. Vestiges remained. But the Stephenson scandal and the exposés of Klan political corruption spread like a plague from Indiana east, west, and north, across the realms where the now-disgraced Grand Dragon had once been a charismatic organizer and a symbol of patriotism and Christian virtue.

Whatever was left of the empire was seldom invisible. As public concern grew over the invasion of political processes by a secret society, state after state had passed antimask laws. Klansmen could still parade if they wanted to, but no longer with hoods to hide their faces.

In the South strong roots remained, but violence by Klan extremists against both blacks and whites had turned increasing numbers of people against the entire movement. Nationally, internal dissensions and power struggles had taken their toll. At the same time, the public emotions that had fueled the Klan—the flag-waving frenzy left over from World War I, reaction against Jazz Age morality and the Demon Rum, fear that the Pope of Rome was about to take over America—were subsiding. The Klan had provided an outlet for these tensions, and now the pressure was running low.

Of its professed goals, the Klan in Indiana, as elsewhere, had achieved virtually nothing. Repeated efforts to contain the "Catholic menace" in the school system through new teacher curriculum requirements had failed in the Klan-dominated legislature of 1925, largely because of factional divisions and the machinations of the Grand Dragon himself. Catholic businessmen had suffered boycotts. But by 1927 they were recovering and the "TWK" (Trade With a Klansman) signs were long gone from the windows of their competitors.

Despite raids by the Klan's Horse Thief Detectives, bootleggers continued to make profits through the 1920s. By the end of 1933, the Klan's cherished Prohibition amendment had been repealed and the Demon Rum would soon be again plentiful and legal. In June 1933, popularly elected delegates to an Indiana constitutional convention ratified the Twenty-first (repeal) Amendment by a vote of 246 to 83.

Brothels, another Klan target, never really disappeared, save in a few small towns. By the 1930s, whorehouses were again flourishing in Indianapolis day and night, some only a fifteen-minute walk from the state capitol and many at the Depression rate of two dollars a trick. During national conventions or sessions of the state legislature, prices went up and reinforcements, often subsidized by political lobbyists, came in from out of town to set up business in downtown hotel rooms. Gambling continued in dives and elsewhere. Slot machines abounded in private clubs like the Indianapolis Press Club. City officials who came there for lunch and contacts were often among the players.

The Klan had made greater impact on the negative side. It had cost anti-Klan Protestant pastors their jobs, as in the case of the Reverend Trusty in Indianapolis. It had cost the Indiana Republican party most of the staunch support

183

of black voters it had enjoyed since Lincoln's day. Niblack, an anti-Klan Republican, said:

> One lasting result [of the Klan] was the alienation of 90 per cent of the Negro vote from the [Indiana] Republican Party. . . . When Stephenson used the Republican Party to nominate and elect Klan Governors, Legislators, Judges, Mayors and other officials, the word got around. In 1924 when Ed Jackson, Stephenson's candidate for Governor, was elected, the 5th and 6th Wards in Indianapolis, Negro Wards along Indiana Avenue, went Democratic for the first time.[1]

The Klan had tarnished politics in general. Even those politicians of either major party who had ever had any contact with the Invisible Empire would long suffer when their connections were brought up. It had caused often-bitter dissensions in churches and clubs. Many posts of the American Legion had split on the Klan issue. Even families became divided over the Klan. In their *Middletown* study, the Lynds tell of one husband's reason for his divorce: "She and I split up over the G—D— Klan. I couldn't stand them around any longer."[2]

Enough of the Klan antipapist spirit survived to be a major factor in the defeat of Catholic Al Smith in his 1928 bid for the presidency. But by 1930, the national membership of more than five million once claimed by the Invisible Empire had dropped to under 300,000, mostly in the South.

Then, as the Depression spread across the land, what remained of the Klan offered no solutions or hope for the growing millions of unemployed. Even if it had, few could spare the ten-dollar initiation fee, plus six to seven dollars for a robe. By the 1940s, America was again at war. The Pope as the nation's perceived enemy was largely forgotten as Americans united against more real enemies—the warlords of Japan and the Nazi barbarians of Germany.

Still, Klan or no Klan, strong currents of racism persisted in American life. In 1943, in the midst of the war effort, race riots erupted in Detroit, where new waves of blacks and whites from the South had come to work in war industries. Thirty-four people were killed and hundreds injured before troops came in to quell the disorders.

Racism continued in the military. Black and white troops were still segregated, and blacks were routinely relegated to menial jobs. Black officers could not enter white officers' clubs. In England there were even lynchings of black soldiers by their white fellow Americans because the blacks had dated white English girls.

It was this same racism that, in the 1950s and 1960s, brought forth a new Ku Klux Klan in the South of its Reconstruction, white supremacist origins. It was smaller but more violent than any of its predecessors. This new one-track, paranoid-racist Klan became the terrorist guerrilla wing of the South's massive resistance to a new age of civil rights for blacks.

As early as 1953, a new, small Klan group called, redundantly, the U.S. Klans, Knights of the Ku Klux Klan, had been formed in Atlanta by an auto plant worker named Eldon Edwards. He had little success until about two years later, after a U.S. Supreme Court decision and follow-up court mandate had sent shock waves through the white supremacist South.

The first alarm sounded on May 17, 1954, when the court outlawed racial segregation in public schools. (Ironically, the decision came not on a case from the Deep South, but from Topeka, Kansas, which had long maintained separate elementary schools for blacks and whites.) The aftershock came in 1955 when the court mandated that racial desegregation of public school proceed "with all deliberate speed."

With these threats to white supremacy growing, in September 1956 Edwards attracted some three thousand to a Klan rally on Stone Mountain, near Atlanta, where Colonel Simmons had started his Invisible Empire more than forty years earlier. Within two years, an estimated fifteen thousand had joined his new Klan.

Edwards died in 1960, but more powerful leaders took over. One of the largest of the new groups was the United

Klans of America, organized by Robert Shelton, an Alabama salesman. The United Klans soon became a sort of loosely knit empire across the South. By 1965, Klan membership had grown to between thirty-five and fifty thousand.[3]

Southern political leaders, while not openly endorsing the Klan, helped create the climate for its growth. On January 19, 1956, the Alabama State Legislature passed a "nullification" resolution, asserting a state's right to negate Supreme Court rulings in its jurisdiction. On February 21 of the same year—again hearkening back more than a century and a half to the "interposition" and "nullification" resolutions drafted by Thomas Jefferson and James Madison against the Alien and Sedition acts[4]—the Virginia State Legislature passed another "interposition resolution," claiming a state's right to interpose its sovereignty against enactments or rulings from the federal government.

Both turned out to be empty political gestures. But in March 1956, a call by 101 southern congressmen for "massive resistance" to the school desegregation order "by all lawful means" inspired a broader audience. Southern politicians began wearing "Never!" (to school integration) labels on their coat labels. "White Citizens Councils" began organizing to put economic and social pressures on any supporters of, or even moderates on, new civil rights for blacks.

The school integration battles were only part of the picture. As new civil rights laws and court rulings came from Washington, D.C., the South felt increasingly besieged. In 1956, the Supreme Court banned racially segregated seating on city buses in Birmingham, Alabama, after a year-long boycott by blacks brought a test case. In 1960, in a case from Virginia, the Supreme Court outlawed racial segregation in interstate bus terminals. In 1964, in a sweeping "omnibus" Civil Rights Act, Congress outlawed racial discrimination in a broad spectrum of American life—public accommodations, housing, jobs, and public services. In 1965, a new Voting Rights Act, strongly promoted by President Lyndon Johnson, authorized federal officials to supervise voter registration in states where blacks had been systematically blocked from the registration rolls.

The South fought back on legal grounds but repeatedly lost. Resistance to race mixing by lawful means was clearly not working, and nowhere was this fact more challenging than in the minds of the new Klan. In such a climate the new Klan grew and its violence escalated. From 1956 to 1966, there were more than one thousand documented cases of racist terrorism, assaults, and murders committed by Klansmen and their allies.[5] The victims were both black and white.

In May 1961, in Anniston, Alabama, Klansmen led a white gang that firebombed the first Freedom Riders bus, where blacks and whites had joined to test the new bus terminal desegregation ruling, and later beat them when they arrived on a second bus in Birmingham. The nation was shocked when, in September 1963, four young black girls were killed in a bomb explosion in their church in Birmingham. The girls, one eleven and three fourteen, were in a room adjoining an outside wall where Klansmen had planted a dynamite bomb. Shortly after the bombing, a white supremacist was quoted as telling a group of Klansmen that the men who planted the bomb deserved medals. The girls in the church, he said, were "just little niggers . . . and if there's four less niggers tonight, then I say, 'good for whoever planted the bomb.' "[6]

Despite new federal laws, killing was still a state crime to be prosecuted in state courts. In case after case, accused Klan or allied racist killers went free in trials before all-white southern juries. Tom Coleman, a part-time deputy sheriff who admitted shooting Jonathan Daniels, a white civil rights worker in Fort Deposit, Alabama, in 1965, was indicted for manslaughter, but it took an all-white jury only two hours to acquit him.

Two Klansmen who shot and killed Lieutenant Colonel Lemuel Penn, a black army reserve officer, as he drove through Georgia on his return trip to Washington, D.C., were identified by the driver of the Klan car from which they fired. They were charged with the killing, but they were also acquitted by another all-white jury.

Other cases never even came to trial. The F.B.I. investigated the dynamite bombing of the Birmingham church where the four young black girls were killed. An eyewitness told them he had seen Klansmen plant the bomb. Still, no one was charged. It was fourteen years later before the case was reopened by Alabama attorney-general William Baxley. By then the social and legal climate had changed somewhat. A seventy-nine-year-old Klansman named Robert Chambliss was charged with first-degree murder in the bombing, found guilty by a jury, and sentenced to life. More than one Klansman had obviously been involved, but no one else was ever charged in the bombing case.

The disappearance of three civil rights workers in Mississippi in 1964 attracted national attention. An investigation by the F.B.I., along with federal reward money, finally produced information that their bodies were buried in an earthen dam near Philadelphia, Mississippi. Michael Schwerner and Andrew Goodman, both white and from New York, and James Chaney, who was black, had, as later revealed, been shot to death by Klansmen with the connivance of a deputy sheriff.

Still, no state murder charges were brought. It was only when the U.S. Justice Department called a federal grand jury into the case that indictments charging civil rights violations were secured against nineteen men, including Klansmen and their deputy sheriff accomplice. Seven were convicted in the killings, but only on federal civil rights violations. The murders were proved, but the maximum sentence any of the accused could, and did, receive under the federal law was ten years in prison for "conspiracy to violate civil rights."

The case of Viola Liuzzo in Alabama in 1965 was even

more illustrative of the reluctance of the besieged white supremacist South to deal with Klan racist killers. Mrs. Liuzzo, a thirty-nine-year-old white housewife and mother from Detroit, had gone to Alabama in March 1965 to help blacks in their second march from Selma. She had volunteered to shuttle loads of blacks in her car for the march. On the night of March 25, she was driving back to Montgomery to pick up more black marchers, accompanied by a young black man, Leroy Moton.

On a desolate stretch of road in Lowndes County, her car was pursued and overtaken by a carload of Klansmen. As the Klan car pulled alongside, Mrs. Liuzzo looked to see who had been following her. From the back seat of the Klan car a man fired two shots from a .38 caliber pistol, killing Mrs. Liuzzo instantly. Moton escaped further harm by feigning death.

Three Klansmen—Eugene Thomas, William Orville Eaton, and Collie Leroy Wilkins—were indicted for the murder. The state's case against them was strong. Moton described how they had been pursued. More important, one passenger in the Klan car was an undercover F.B.I. agent who said he had seen Wilkins fire the fatal shots.

In Wilkins's murder trial in May 1965, his defense attorney, Klan "Imperial Klonsel" Matt Murphy, Jr., brought forth no witness to discredit the eyewitness testimony. Instead, in his summation to the jury, he delivered a long, antiblack, anti-Semitic, anti-Communist harangue that exploited the depths of southern redneck racism:

> And this white woman who got killed? White woman? Where's that NAACP card? I thought I'd never see the day when Communists and niggers and white niggers and Jews were flying under the banner of the United Nations flag, not the American flag we fought for.
>
> I'm proud to be a white man and I'm proud that I stand up on my feet for white supremacy. Not black supremacy, not the mixing and mongrelization of the races . . . not the Zionists that run that bunch of niggers. The white people

are not gonna run before them. And when white people join up to 'em them become white niggers.

Do you know those big black niggers were driven by the woman, sitting right in the back seat? Niggers! One white woman and these niggers. Right there. Riding right through your county. Communists dominate them niggers.

You know what that nigger [Moton] said on the stand. No. Yeah. No. Yeah. Like a 10-year-old boy. He should have been saying Yes, Sir, and No, Sir before that honorable white judge. But the buck hasn't got the sense, the morals, or the decency.

I said now look, boy. Look down at your feets. Niggers only understand this kind of talk. How many feets away was that car? So he looked down at his feet and said about 25 feet away. . . . He said he passed out for 25–30 minutes. . . . What's he doing down there all that time? In that car *alone* with that woman.

Then the nigger ran up the road and a truck came by and he stopped it. There was a rabbi in that truck. A rabbi. Of course he stopped and put the nigger in the back. And there they were—rabbi with a nigger . . . white woman, nigger man, nigger woman—all in there, feet to feet.

Integration breaks every moral law God ever wrote. Noah's son was Ham and committed adultery and was banished and his sons were Hamites and God banished them and they went to Africa and the only thing they ever built was grass huts. No white woman can ever marry a descendant of Ham. That's God's law. . . . I don't care what Lyndon Johnson or anybody else says.

After ten hours deliberation, the jury announced that it was hopelessly deadlocked. A retrial was ordered. In the second trial in October 1965, it took another white jury only two hours to find Wilkins and his fellow Klansmen not guilty of either murder or conspiracy.

Again, the federal government moved in. Wilkins,

Thomas, and Eaton were indicted and tried on federal charges of conspiring to violate civil rights. They were found guilty and sentenced to ten years in prison for a crime that in other areas could have brought Wilkins the death penalty.

Violent and determined as it seemed, the new southern Klan's guerrilla war—along with the rest of the South's "massive resistance"—against new equality for blacks was doomed from the start. It is more than a cliché to say that civil rights for American blacks was a long-delayed idea whose time had come.

By the 1980s, blacks and whites would be sharing schoolrooms, bus seats, hotels, and restaurants on an equal basis, in both North and South. By federal law, banks would have signs at their counters advising customers not only that they could not discriminate on the basis of race, religion, or national origin, but also that they could appeal if they believed their rights had been violated. Companies advertising for help would proclaim that they were equal opportunity employers, even if they didn't always follow through. Black men would become mayors of major cities: Atlanta, Baltimore, New York, and, in one less fortunate case, Washington, D.C.[7] In Virginia in 1989, a grandson of black slaves, L. Douglas Wilder, became governor.

Still, laws and political victories could not erase the persisting currents of racism in American life. Millions of whites, in both North and South, while accepting the idea of equal rights for blacks, were still not ready to accept them as social equals. Despite equal opportunity employers, blacks complained they were often the last to be hired and first to be fired. Racism itself, however, had gone underground. In public life, in mainline politics, in business and advertising, it had become a sensitive area to be avoided at all costs.

When David Duke, a racist and former Klansman, won a Republican seat in the Louisiana State Legislature in 1988, mainline Republican leaders rushed to disavow both him and the Klan. When he sought the Republican nomination for the U.S. Senate in the 1990 Louisiana primary election, Republican leaders again disavowed him and supported his Democratic opponent. Duke lost, but, campaigning in a lower key, calling for reforms in the affirmative action program and more equality of opportunity for whites, he managed to get 44 percent of the total vote and 60 percent of the white vote.

When Andy Rooney, a satirist on CBS-TV's "60 Minutes" show, was quoted in a Los Angeles gay magazine as having made denigrating remarks about "black genes" and reproductivity, CBS hastened to announce that he had been dismissed from the show, even though Rooney said he was misquoted.[8] (He was rehired about a month later.)

Meanwhile, estimated total Klan membership, which had climbed to forty-two-thousand at the height of the civil rights battles in 1965, had dropped to about fifteen hundred in 1974. By 1981 it rose again to an estimated eleven thousand, but by 1988 it had dropped again to about five thousand.[9]

The ups and downs seemed to coincide with changes in the American social and legal climate. The first dramatic drop came after the Klan had clearly lost its battle to stop racial integration in the late 1960s and early 1970s. The resurgence was at least in part a rally on new fronts with broader targets: affirmative action for blacks, Vietnamese fishermen, gay rights, "Jewish conspiracies" . . .

The drop-off of nearly 50 percent by 1988 coincided with a growing public revulsion against Klan bigotry and violence and the better police work and stronger legal action that followed. Between 1979 and 1985, the U.S. Justice Department prosecuted at least eighty-four Klansmen for racially motivated violence.[10] At the state level, juries were no longer reluctant to convict Klan members for criminal acts.

In addition, entire Klan organizations were being held legally responsible for the acts of their members. Klansmen had been convicted on criminal charges for the 1981 lynching of a black youth—Michael Donald—in Mobile, Alabama. But in a civil suit that followed—brought by the Southern Poverty Law Center of Montgomery, Alabama—their parent group, the United Klans of America, was ordered in 1987 to pay seven million dollars in damages to Michael Donald's mother. The United Klans didn't have such money, of course, but continued seizure of their assets put serious restrictions on their activities. Despite anonymous threats on his life, Morris Dees, the courageous attorney of the law center's Klanwatch project continued to fight organizers and inciters of racist violence. They suffered an even heavier blow in 1990 for their alleged responsibility in the killing of Mulugeta Seraw, an Ethiopian student beaten to death by Skinheads in Portland, Oregon, in 1988. The convicted Skinheads—members of one of several gangs of disaffected youth being recruited in northern cities by white-supremacist extremists—said they had been organized and encouraged by agents of the White Aryan Resistance and two of its leaders, Tom and John Metzger.

In a subsequent damage suit brought by the Southern Poverty Law Center and the Anti-Defamation League of B'nai B'rith, the Metzgers, their Aryan Resistance group, and two Skinheads were ordered to pay twelve and one half million dollars in damages to Seraw's family. They had not even a fraction of this amount, but seizure of their available assets was expected to continue.

Names of the continuing Klan groups varied. The United Klans of America continued as a sort of umbrella group for several other units. But, increasingly, the Klan became a magnet for violent affiliated racist groups spreading into the North and Northwest. Aryan Nations, White Aryan Resistance, The Order, The Brotherhood, Skinheads. Whatever their names or organizational structures, however, they were inevitably fixed in the public mind as branches of the Ku Klux Klan, whose name itself had become anathema, even among Americans who shared many of its racial prejudices. Few Americans could be expected to join or support a Klan whose members were known to have infiltrated military posts in North Carolina—the Marine base at Camp LeJeune and army installations at Fort Bragg—to steal rifles, ammunition, and grenades—apparently for a coming race war, or perhaps a revolution against ZOG—the Zionist Occupational Government—in Washington, D.C. In other areas, members of Klan-leaning, neo-Nazi groups like Aryan Nations or The Order had been arrested and convicted of armed robberies to finance their cause.

The "100 percent American" Klan that had once rallied Middle America in defense of flag and Christian virtue was long gone. It had been split by the ambitions and infighting of its leaders, shattered in 1925 by the greed and lusts of an oversexed Grand Dragon, and finally swallowed up in the Great Depression and World War II. What remained of the Klan in the 1990s had become only the nucleus of a paranoid fringe of American society, self-destructing through the crime and violence of its own rank-and-file.

L'Envoi: Onward Christian Soldiers

AS THE KU KLUX KLAN'S Invisible Empire lay dying in the late 1920s, some dedicated Klansmen clung to hopes that some new rally would restore and carry on what they believed were the true Klan ideals of patriotism and virtue.

In 1927, in a book denouncing the leaders—especially D. C. Stephenson—that he felt had betrayed and destroyed his organization, Edgar Allen Booth wrote:

> Let us love and cherish, if we will, the fiery cross and the memory of the white-clad Christians who marched with their heads erect as the strains of 'Onward Christian Soldiers' floated out upon the night air. . . . Let us form an organization in which true Americanism will prevail, in fact as well as in theory. . . . Let us lift bodily upon the wreck of the Ku Klux Klan those principles which are so clearly loved. Let us choose for our criteria that which the Klan chose, Christ.[1]

Booth's hopes were obviously wishful thinking. In the more than sixty years since he wrote those words, no single organization with the unity, emotional appeal, or power of his "white-clad Christians" had appeared on the American scene.

195

Still, for many Americans the appeal of the flag, pure Americanism, and conservative moral and social values remained strong forces. And once again, as in the 1920s, they felt threatened by unsettling, sometimes shocking, new social and moral trends: widespread court-sanctioned abortion, legalized pornography, open homosexuality, out-lawing of prayers and the Pledge of Allegiance in schools, obscene music lyrics, growing crime, drugs, flag burning . . .

At about the same time, there was in many areas a growing uneasiness about a trend that had been one of the concerns distorted and exploited by the 1920s Klan—new waves of immigration and increasing birth rates of "alien" people, now notably Asian and Hispanic; a fear of being engulfed by a population other than "our kind of people."

In many ways the picture resembled the collage of forces—racial, religious, patriotic and moral—that had fu-eled the 1920s Klan. But, unlike the Klan, the organiza-tions opposing new trends were themselves a diverse mix-ture of forces, ranging from fundamentalists of the Religious Right to hawkish flag-wavers, many of whom never went to any church; from self-appointed moralistic censors of schoolbooks and television shows to get-tough-on-crime law-and-order crusaders; from nativistic English-as-our-official-language proponents to Klan-inspired ex-tremists who threatened Vietnamese fishermen on the Texas coast.

Scattered in between were masses of ordinary Americans who, while not especially concerned with such religious fundamentalist worries as secular humanism in school-books or the teaching of evolution in science classes, still felt things were going awry in their country. They felt something should be done, but still hadn't brought it into focus.

The diverse racist, nativist, and religious forces in the 1920s had awaited only some means of unification and direction to become the Ku Klux Klan. Obviously the paranoid, violent, sometimes criminal fringe calling itself the Klan in the 1990s would not provide this direction at the patriotic and moral level. The closest thing to direction seemed to come from the growing political activism of the so-called Religious Right. But it, too, was more of a collage than a unified organization.

Its organizations varied in names, strength, and major targets: the Moral Majority, Concerned Women for America, National Association of Christian Educators, the Christian Coalition. Even the Religious Right's television evangelists, who through the 1980s reaped millions of dollars from their armchair audiences, represented no specific organization. And by 1990, their image had been tarnished by the fall from grace, through sexual misadventures, of such apostles as Jimmy Swaggart and Jim Bakker.

However, for those who felt, or feared, that some new version of the 1920s Klan was in the offing, surface analogies abounded. In the 1920s a Klan newspaper editor had expressed a dominant sentiment when he wrote, [the Klan] "is going to bring clean motion pictures to this country; it is going to bring clean literature to this country." Today's Religious Right and its allies have multiplied censorship efforts, monitoring television shows and calling for boycotts of sponsors of shows they feel are immoral or anti-Christian.

The 1920s Klan called for Protestant Christian government. As Klan Imperial Klokard (a Klan traveling lecturer) William James Mahoney had said, "We magnify the Bible as the basis of our Constitution, the source of our laws." Through the 1980s new Religious Right activists were doing the same, sometimes swinging the balance to defeat political candidates who didn't go along. In a 1986 public letter, Connecticut's Senator Lowell Weicker, Jr., said: "In the past few years I've seen many members of Congress attacked viciously and defeated for public office because they dared disagree with a fundamentalists' view of proper voting in a 'Christian nation'."

Then, as now, schools appear as a major target. The Klan opposed the teaching of evolution and supported legally mandated prayers in public schools. (As noted earlier, the

Klan's call for separation of church and state meant only separation of the Catholic church from the state.) Today's fundamentalist evangelicals demand equal time for creationism along with evolution in science classes. They denounce court rulings banning school prayers, call for a Constitutional amendment to get around the First Amendment's prohibition of establishment of religion, and propose religious tests for judicial nominees to get "God back into the classroom."

In the 1920s, the Klan feared un-American Catholic influence in the nation's schools and sought legislation to restrict it through new laws on teacher certification and curriculum requirements. In Oregon, the Klan and its allies pushed a law through the state legislature that would have required all students, including Catholics, in grades one through six to attend public schools. It was, however, declared unconstitutional before it could take effect. In the 1980s, fundamentalists of the Religious Right turned their guns on secular humanism, especially books and curricula that taught, or indicated, that people can make informed choices on life and values through their own reason as much as through divine direction.

At another level, and perhaps with broader support, various moralistic activist groups, especially Beverly La Haye's Concerned Women for America, attacked sex education courses. And at one extreme even new math courses came under fire because they did not give children a sense of absolutes and could in some way lead to "situational morality."

They scored some local, if limited, victories. Some jittery school boards removed books from school libraries without even consulting teachers. And in Alabama in 1981, fundamentalist parents groups forced the removal of several textbooks from the state-approved school reading list on charges of anti-Christian secular humanism. Court battles followed, with one federal district judge upholding the ban on the grounds that secular humanism was itself a religion

and therefore inadmissible in public school curricula. He
was later overruled on appeal.

Religious Right pressures on schools continued into the
1990s, with a goal set by Robert Simonds, founder of Citizens for Excellence in Education, which became a network
of local activist groups of the National Association of Christian Educators: "We have a plan to take our entire education system back and put it into God's hands. The way we
are going to do it is to take control of every school board in
America."[2]

Despite local and regional activism, Religious Right fundamentalists were still a small minority. Their venture into
national politics with Pat Robertson as a choice for the
1988 Republican presidential nomination was a resounding
failure. In the early Iowa caucuses Robertson did come in a
surprisingly high second, not far behind Bob Dole. But in
primary elections across the nation his vaunted "silent
army" turned out to be no more than scattered platoons.

Still, masses of nonfundamentalists, ordinary Americans, felt uneasy with what they saw as a growing moral,
social, and cultural chaos. In the 1920s the flag-waving
fever left over from World War I looked for some new outlet,
which many found in the Klan. By the 1990s, with communism fading as an enemy of Americanism, many felt the
cold warriors of the far Right would also be looking for new
outlets and rallying points to enlarge their numbers.

Could a new Religious Right, minority though it was,
emerge as the nucleus for a broader organization with a
solution for the nation's moral and social ills? Could it
somehow blend its narrowly defined view of Christianity
with patriotic, nativistic, and law-and-order appeals, fuse
with other far Right groups and become, under a new name,
another Klanlike force in American life?

As the nation entered the final decade of the twentieth
century, some thought it possible. Both the Religious Right
and the political far Right continued pressure at regional
and local levels. One far Right ideologue, Paul Weyrich,
president of the Free Congress Foundation, an ultraconser-

vative think tank in Washington, D.C., saw this as the best path to power. "We will only be powerful in Washington," he said, "when we once again speak for a powerful movement outside Washington—when we have taken the countryside."[3]

Was the countryside ready to be taken? It was not impossible but seemed highly unlikely. The provincial countryside where the Klan got its foothold in the 1920s was a far cry from the mobile, technological, entertainment-surfeited countryside of the 1990s. Television was then still decades away. Airplanes and radios were still novelties. In Indiana the Klan attracted many, if not most, of its new members at all-day outings, picnics, or barbecues. Often these were only diversions in town.

In the 1920s, nativistic flag-waving, along with racism, was taken for granted by most Middle Americans. Today these forces persist but, largely due to vast, instant communications networks, they are more quickly and openly scrutinized and debated, and they are often put down.

The postwar America of the 1920s, flanked by two still-protective oceans, was dominantly isolationist. We had proved our valor in France, but now we were home again to stay. We were something special and separate and wanted to remain that way. But after emerging from World War II as a world power, America came, inevitably, into the mainstream of world history and world responsibilities. Even concern for 100 percent Americanism went far beyond our shores, with billions of dollars and thousands of soldiers' lives invested to promote or protect our concept of freedom and democracy and economic opportunity around the globe.

At home, for the masses of ordinary Americans of the type once attracted to the Klan, the plethora of Religious Right and far Right groups suffered from an identity problem. Along with its crusades to save America, the Klan had offered recognizable, unifying forces: mystical symbolism, secret rites, special regalia hoods, robes, flaming crosses, and even a special language. Today's activist far Right offers no such attractions, no costumes, no special insignia, nothing to give a special sense of belonging.

Could some new master salesman, perhaps some new D. C. Stephenson, fill this void? Could some new organization—with a new name, new symbols and perhaps even new regalia—arise to rally and exploit Middle America in another misguided patriotic and moral crusade?

By the 1990s, none had appeared. Yet if it came one might share the view of Robert Coughlan:

> "When some new bogey arises on Main Street to take the place of the pope, and some new organization arises to take the place of the Klan, one can only hope that the new generation will turn out to be less ignorant than the old."[4]

Appendix: Klan Nomenclature

THE NOMENCLATURE, language and titles used by the Ku Klux Klan had an air of mystery that gave its members a special sense of secret comradeship and its officers an aura of power. Some of the words came from the Klan of the Reconstruction South, but most were invented by its successor's first organizer, William J. Simmons, and his associates after 1915. Following is a partial list of words and terms used by Klansmen throughout their many realms.

Ayak "Are you a Klansman?" A secret query to determine if one is talking to a fellow Klan member or not.

Akia "A Klansman I am." (After this affirmative reply the other would reply *Kigy,* "Klansman, I greet you," and a *klonversation* followed.)

Domain A Klan unit comprising a group of states. This was probably in existence only during 1921 and 1922.

Emperor This was a special title set up for William J. Simmons after he was retired and succeeded as Imperial Wizard by Hiram W. Evans in 1922.

Exalted Cyclops   Leader of a local Klan chapter elected by members for a one-year term.

Furies   Seven advisors to a Great Titan, head of a Klan province.

Genii   Twelve officers forming the cabinet of the Imperial Wizard.

Grand   This was a prefix meaning an official of a state organization (e.g., the Grand Klabee was the state Klan treasurer).

Grand Dragon   Chief executive of a state Klan—or Realm—appointed for a one-year term by the Imperial Wizard.

Grand Goblin   Head of a multi-state regional Klan district, or Domain.

Great   This prefix applied to officers of the Klan district organizations within a state (e.g., a Great Titan was head of the district unit, appointed either by the Grand Dragon or Imperial Wizard).

Hydras   Nine staff members assisting the state's Grand Dragon.

Imperial   This preceded the titles of various officers and units at Klan national headquarters in Atlanta. At the top was the Imperial Wizard.

Imperial Klonvocation   The national convention of the Klan, held every two years. In the 1920s such meetings occurred in 1922, 1924, and 1926. Those attending included all Klan national officials, state and district officers, and one other delegate from each state and district organization.

Junior Klan   Local organization for Klansmen's children over age twelve.

Kamelia   The Klan organization for women founded by the

first Imperial Wizard, William J. Simmons, after his retirement in 1922. It was soon eclipsed by the new Women of the Ku Klux Klan, supported by the new Imperial Wizard, Hiram W. Evans.

Kigy "Klansman, I greet you."

King Kleagle The chief organizer or recruiter for the Klan in any one state.

Klabee The Klan treasurer at various levels, ranging from simply Klabee for local units to Imperial Klabee in Atlanta headquarters.

Klaliff Klan vice-president at various levels.

Klanton County Klan organization.

Klavern Indoor meeting place of local Klan units.

Kleagle Klan field organizer or recruiter working in the organization of the King Kleagle.

Klectoken The ten-dollar initiation fee paid by a new Klan member.

Kligrapp Klan secretary at various unit levels.

Klokard A traveling Klan lecturer.

Kloncilium The Klan's top executive and judicial council.

Klonversation Conversation between two Klansmen, beginning with secret acronyms for identification.

Klonsel Klan attorney or legal adviser at various levels.

Kloran Ritual book used in Klan initiations and at the beginning and end of meetings.

Kludd Chaplain at various Klan levels.

Kluxing Word often used by Kleagles to describe their recruiting work in specific areas. (It was often used by others, as when D. C. Stephenson told one gathering,

"We're going to Klux Indiana like it's never been Kluxed before.")

Konklave   Any gathering of Klansmen.

Nighthawk   A sort of investigator and watchdog, who checked the character of prospective Klan members and their later conduct. Each local unit of the Klan had one.

Province   A Klan group of counties, under the direction of a Great Titan.

Queens of the Golden Mask   One of the Klan's women's organizations, along with *Kamelia* and *Women of the Ku Klux Klan*.

Realm   The Klan organization of a state, established after a certain number of local Klan chapters had been chartered by national headquarters.

Sanbog   "Strangers are near. Be on guard." Warning issued during a Klonversation between Klansmen.

Terrors   Eleven elected members of the staff of the Exalted Cyclops of a local Klan chapter.

Titan   Head of a Klan province, or district organization covering several local Klan chapters.

Wizard   National Klan chief executive, i.e., Imperial Wizard.

Notes

Introduction: The Realm of the Dragon

1. Robert Coughlan, "Konklave in Kokomo," in *The Aspirin Age: 1919–1941,* ed. Isabel Leighton (Simon and Schuster: New York, 1949), 115.

2. Membership figures for secret societies like the Klan are necessarily hard to confirm, and Klan leaders tended to exaggerate. In Indiana the leading Klan publication, the *Fiery Cross,* reported a circulation of 100,000 and an estimated total membership at about 500,000. Later, just before the Klan's huge tristate rally on July 4, 1923, in Kokomo, *Fiery Cross* editor Milton Elrod told reporters that charters would be issued to ninety-three Indiana Klan units representing 400,000 Klansmen (*Indianapolis Times,* 4 July 1923). Later official investigations brought figures ranging from 125,000 to those keeping up dues "in good standing" to over 400,000. Most students of the Klan movement seem to have accepted 250,000 to 300,000 as the best estimate of Indiana Klan membership.

3. John Moffatt Mecklin, *The Ku Klux Klan: A Study of the American Mind* (New York: Harcourt, Brace, 1924), 96.

4. Ibid., 13.

5. H. L. Mencken and George Jean Nathan, *Smart Set* (February 1923): editorial.

6. H. L. Mencken and George Jean Nathan, *Smart Set* (March 1923): editorial.

7. Irving Leibowitz, *My Indiana* (Englewood Cliffs, N.J.: Prentice Hall, 1964): 211.

8. William Peirce Randel, *The Ku Klux Klan—A Century of Infamy* (Philadelphia, New York: Chilton, 1965), ix.

9. Frank Bohn, "The Ku Klux Klan Interpreted," *American Journal of Sociology* (January 1925) 30: 385–407.

10. Ruth Miller Elson, *Guardians of Tradition: American Schoolbooks of the Nineteenth Century* (Lincoln, Nebraska: University of Nebraska Press, 1964), 340.

11. Hiram Wesley Evans, "The Klan of Tomorrow," in William Miller, *A New History of the United States* (New York: Braziller, 1958), 355–56.

12. Lothrop Stoddard was identified as Exalted Cyclops of Provisional Klan No. 1 in Massachusetts by *Hearst's Magazine*. Despite his denials, the periodical claimed to have supporting evidence. Noted in David M. Chalmers's *Hooded Americanism* (Garden City, N.Y.: 1965), 270–71.

13. "Rise and Fall of the K.K.K.," *New Republic* (November 30, 1927): unsigned editorial.

14. Editor Billie Mayfield in *Colonel Mayfield's Weekly*, Houston, Tex., quoted in Arnold S. Rice, *The Ku Klux Klan in American Politics* (New York: Haskell House, 1972), 24–25.

15. Arnold S. Rice, *The Ku Klux Klan in American Politics* (New York: Haskell House, 1972), 15.

16. Leibowitz, *My Indiana*, 190–91.

17. David M. Chalmers, *Hooded Americanism* (Garden City, New York, Doubleday and Co., 1965) 113.

18. Ibid.

19. Norman F. Weaver, "The Knights of the Ku Klux Klan in Wisconsin, Indiana, Ohio and Michigan" (Ph.D. diss., University of Wisconsin, 1954), 153–54.

20. Chalmers, *Hooded Americanism*, 165.

21. Hiram Wesley Evans, "The Klan's Fight for Americanism," *North American Review*, (March, 1926).

22. *Noblesville Daily Ledger*, 21 November 1925.

1. Evansville: Bridgehead on the Ohio

1. *Evansville Courier*, 6 May 1920.

2. *Evansville Courier*, 1 May 1920.

3. Chalmers, *Hooded Americanism*, 30.

4. Mecklin, *Ku Klux Klan: A Study*, 9.

5. Chalmers, *Hooded Americanism*, 32–33.

6. Ibid., 38.

7. E. H. Loucks, *The Ku Klux Klan in Pennsylvania* (Harrisburg, Pa.: Telegraph Press, 1936), 23.

8. *Evansville Courier*, 27 March 1922.

9. This and following quotes in *Evansville Courier*, 10 June 1922.

10. Frank Luther Mott, *American Journalism: A History, 1690–1960* (New York: Macmillan, 1962), 730–31.

11. *Evansville Courier*, 9 June 1922.

2. Steve: Birth of a Salesman

1. John Bartlow Martin, *Indiana: An Interpretation* (New York: Alfred A. Knopf, 1947), 185.

2. Samuel Taylor Moore, "How the Kleagles Collected the Cash," *Independent* (13 December 1924): 517.

3. Weaver, "Klan in Wisconsin, Indiana . . .", 149.

4. Edgar Allen Booth, *The Mad Mullah of America* (Columbus, Ohio: Boyd Ellison, 1927), 155.

5. Moore, "Kleagles Collected," 517.

6. Morton Harrison, "Gentlemen from Indiana," *Atlantic Monthly*, (May 1928).

7. Rice, *Klan in Politics*, 9.

8. Robert A. Butler, *So They Framed Stephenson* (Huntington, Ind: privately published, 1940), 13–14.

9. Weaver, "Klan in Wisconsin, Indiana . . .", 169.

10. Alva W. Taylor, "What the Klan Did In Indiana," *New Republic* (16 November 1927).

Notes

11. Booth, *Mad Mullah,* 297.

12. Ibid., 75.

13. Statement issued through F. A. Miller, editor of the *South Bend Tribune,* and reported in the *New York Times* (3 February 1924).

14. Moore, "Kleagles Collected."

15. John L. Niblack, *The Life and Times of a Hoosier Judge* (Greenfield, Ind.: 1973), 196–97.

16. Local, or county, Klan chapters were chartered individually by Klan headquarters. After a certain number in a state had been so chartered, the national Klan set up a formal state organization called a Realm. By the time of the Kokomo rally, at least ninety Indiana Klan county chapters were said to have been officially chartered.

17. Coughlan, "Konklave in Kokomo," 107–08.

18. Weaver, "Klan in Wisconsin, Indiana . . .", 145.

19. This and Stephenson's reason for being late quoted in Coughlan, "Konklave in Kokomo," 106.

20. Allen Safianow, " 'Konklave in Kokomo' Revisited," *Historian* (University of Toledo) 50 (3), (May 1988): 333–34.

3. Target: Rome

1. Mecklin, *Ku Klux Klan: A Study,* 157–58.

2. Francis S. Bethen, S. J., *The Roman Index of Forbidden Books* (St. Louis, Mo., and London: B. Herder, 1917).

3. Henry Steele Commager, *The American Mind* (New Haven: Yale University Press, 1950), 192.

4. Coughlan, "Konklave in Kokomo," 113–14.

5. Robert S. Lynd and Helen M. Lynd, *Middletown* (New York: Harcourt, Brace, 1929) 482.

6. As recounted by Martin in *Indiana,* 192, and by Chalmers in *Hooded Americanism,* 162.

7. Advertisement in the *Kourier,* a Klan publication widely circulated in church circles, quoted by Leibowitz, *My Indiana,* 190.

8. Cited by Weaver, "Klan in Wisconsin, Indiana . . .", 145.

9. Harrison, "Gentlemen from Indiana," 678.

10. Coughlan, "Konklave in Kokomo," 114.

11. Mecklin, *Ku Klux Klan: A Study,* 157.

12. Elson, *Guardians of Tradition,* 48.

13. Ibid., 49.

14. Humphrey J. Desmond, *The Know-Nothing Party,* 109, cited in Mecklin, *Ku Klux Klan: A Study.*

15. *The New Catholic Encyclopedia* (New York: McGraw-Hill, 1967) 4:429.

16. Ibid., 13:854 ff.

17. Ibid., 4:434.

18. Cardinal James Gibbons, *A Retrospect of Fifty Years,* vol. 1, 250, quoted in Mecklin, *Ku Klux Klan: A Study,* 164.

19. Mecklin, *Ku Klux Klan: A Study,* 164.

20. Ibid., 165–66.

21. Archbishop Keane was removed from his post as rector of the Catholic University after more conservative Catholic prelates had represented him to Rome as a divisive liberal who could not maintain unified Catholic support for the university.

22. Mecklin, *Ku Klux Klan: A Study,* 180.

The Dragon and the Cross

4. Growth: The Visible-Invisible Empire

1. *Fiery Cross* (2 February 1923).
2. Coughlan, "Konklave in Kokomo," 115.
3. Lynd and Lynd, *Middletown,* 482.
4. Ibid., 483.
5. *Fiery Cross* (5 January 1924).
6. Lynd and Lynd, *Middletown,* 483.
7. Harrison, "Gentlemen from Indiana."
8. Niblack, *Hoosier Judge,* 190.
9. *Indianapolis News,* 8 October 1926.
10. Moore, "Kleagles Collected," 518.
11. Moore, "Kleagles Collected."
12. Marion Monteval, *The Klan Inside Out,* (Claremore, Okla.: 1924), 53–58.
13. From *The Imperial Knight Hawk,* quoted in Moore "Kleagles Collected."
14. The *Indianapolis Times* of May 26 reported the false alarms came from Maryland and Illinois Streets, Senate Avenue, and St. Clair Streets, and the Meyer-Kaiser Bank Building, all flanking the parade route.
15. *Indianapolis Times,* 4 July 1923.
16. Leibowitz, *My Indiana,* 212.
17. Ibid., 215.
18. Letter from Clay Trusty, Jr., 14 April 1983.
19. Coughlan, "Konklave in Kokomo," 118.
20. Figures cited by Max Bentley, "The Ku Klux Klan in Indiana," *McClure's Magazine* 57 (May 1924).
21. William E. Wilson, "Long Hot Summer in Indiana," *American Heritage* (August 1965), 62.
22. *Indianapolis Times,* 24 February 1927.
23. From articles of impeachment against Judge Dearth filed in Indiana State Legislature, 4 March 1927.
24. *Indianapolis Times,* 24 February 1927.

5. The Military Machine

1. Samuel Tait, Jr., "Indiana," *American Mercury* (April 1926).
2. *Gilliom's Case Against the Indiana Klan,* (State of Indiana Archives, Indiana State Library, Indianapolis). Deposition of D. C. Stephenson.
3. *Indianapolis News,* 7 October 1926.
4. Chalmers, *Hooded Americanism,* 136.
5. Ibid., 199–200.
6. Weaver, "Klan in Wisconsin, Indiana . . .", 212.
7. *Gilliom's Case Against the Indiana Klan.* Testimony of Samuel H. Bemenderfer, Orion Norcross, Edward Stillson, and Thomas W. Swift, 196.
8. Weaver, "Klan in Wisconsin, Indiana . . .", 308–11.
9. Ibid., 217.
10. Ibid., 219.
11. Ibid., 221.
12. Leibowitz, *My Indiana,* 193.
13. Telegram of 12 October 1923 quoted in Randel, *A Century of Infamy,* 211.
14. Moore, "Kleagles Collected."
15. Samuel Taylor Moore, "A Klan Kingdom Collapses," *Independent* (6 December 1924).
16. *Indianapolis News,* 17 December 1924.

Notes

17. *Gilliom's Case against the Indiana Klan*. Deposition of D. C. Stephenson, 99–100.

18. Stanley Frost, "When the Klan Rules," *Outlook* (4 June 1924): 160.

6. Elections: "I Am The Law . . ."

1. *Indianapolis Times,* 25 June 1927.

2. *Indianapolis News,* 12 May 1924.

3. *Indianapolis Star,* 26 May 1924.

4. *Indianapolis News,* 13 May 1924.

5. *Indianapolis News,* 16 January 1924.

6. Leibowitz, *My Indiana,* 189.

7. *Gilliom's Case Against the Klan,* quoted in Weaver, *"Klan in Wisconsin, Indiana . . .",* 207–08.

8. *Gilliom's Case Against the Klan.* Deposition of D. C. Stephenson, 78.

9. Testimony by Warren T. McCray at Marion County, Indiana, bribery trial of Ed Jackson, February 1928.

10. Statement of Warren T. McCray to reporters 10 April 1924, quoted by Niblack, *Hoosier Judge,* 185.

11. *Indianapolis News,* 13 May 1924.

12. *Indianapolis Times* 26 May 1924.

13. Booth, *Mad Mullah,* 24–26.

14. *Indianapolis Times,* 23 May 1924.

15. *Indianapolis Times,* 20 February 1928.

16. *Indianapolis Times,* 13 July 1927.

17. Samuel Taylor Moore, "Consequences of the Klan," *Independent* (30 December 1924).

18. Niblack, *Hoosier Judge,* 192.

19. *Indianapolis News,* 12 May 1924.

20. Wilson, "Hot Summer."

21. *Indianapolis Times,* 30 October 1924.

22. Leibowitz, *My Indiana,* 189–90. The 500,000 figure is no doubt an overstatement.

23. "Link Patterson" was a contrived name for Wilson's actual friend.

24. All following quotes from Wilson, "Hot Summer."

7. A Two-Klan Legislature

1. Niblack, *Hoosier Judge,* 233.

2. The released time bill passed both houses, but was vetoed by Jackson after the attorney-general told him it violated the principle of separation of church and state.

3. Weaver, "Klan in Wisconsin, Indiana . . .", 167–68.

4. Leibowitz, *My Indiana,* 193.

5. Weaver, "Klan in Wisconsin, Indiana . . .", 169.

6. Booth, *Mad Mullah,* 45–46.

7. Willadene Price, *Gutzon Borglum: Artist and Patriot* (Privately published: 1972 edition), 167. Book makes no mention of Klan connections.

8. Booth, *Mad Mullah,* 319–23.

9. Described in letter from Stephenson to Jackson, dated 10 October 1924, reprinted in the *Indianapolis Times,* 15 July 1927.

10. Booth, *Mad Mullah,* 155.

11. *Butler Alumnal Quarterly* (Indianapolis) (April 1925).

The Dragon and the Cross

8. The Ides of March

1. This and other details of Madge Oberholtzer's contacts with Stephenson, including her abduction and rape, are from her "dying declaration," admitted in evidence at Stephenson's trial in Hamilton County Circuit Court, October 1925. Declaration quoted in full in Leibowitz, *My Indiana*, 195–203. Substance of declaration officially on record in files of Indiana Supreme Court, where case was appealed in 1933. (Reports of Cases Decided in the State of Indiana, 16 May 1933 to 22 December 1933, vol. 25, *Stephenson v. State of Indiana*).

2. The Kappas had occupied the house as rental property in 1922 and 1923 before Stephenson bought it from the owner, Mrs. William Graham. Madge had not been a Kappa during her earlier years at Butler, but a Pi Beta Phi. However, she no doubt had Kappa alumnae friends and had possibly visited the house before Stephenson purchased it.

3. Niblack, *Hoosier Judge*, 202.

4. *The Butler Collegian* (Indianapolis) (28 April 1925).

5. *Indianapolis News*, 4 June 1925.

6. Weaver, "Klan in Wisconsin, Indiana . . .", 178.

7. Butler, *They Framed Stephenson*, 23–25.

8. Ibid., 146–47.

9. Niblack, *Hoosier Judge*, 212.

9. The Trial: Murder or Suicide?

1. The arson charges against Klinck and Gentry were finally dropped in October 1927 after Prosecutor William Remy entered a *nolle prosequi* motion. Those against Stephenson and Butler were allowed to expire under the statute of limitations.

2. *Kokomo Dispatch*, 16 November, 1925.

3. Ibid.

4. *Noblesville Ledger*, 17 November, 1925.

10. The "Black Boxes"

1. Weaver, "Klan in Wisconsin, Indiana . . .", 181.

2. Martin, *Indiana*, 198.

3. Weaver, "Klan in Wisconsin, Indiana . . .", 182.

4. *Indianapolis News*, 14 October 1926.

5. *Indianapolis News*, 8 October 1926.

6. *Indianapolis Times*, 15 October 1926.

7. Niblack, *Hoosier Judge*.

11. Appeals: "Hope Springs Eternal . . ."

1. Francis X. Busch, *Guilty or Not Guilty* (Indianapolis & New York: Bobbs-Merrill, 1952), 12.

2. Ibid., 123.

3. Records of appeal available in *Reports of Cases Decided in the Supreme Court of the State of Indiana, May 16, 1933, to December 22, 1933*, 205: 165–82.

4. Butler, *They Framed Stephenson*, 4.

5. Ibid., 14.

6. Ibid., 19–20.

7. Ibid., 21.

8. Ibid., 56.

Notes

9. Affidavit of 27 October 1939, quoted in Butler, *They Framed Stephenson,* 140.

10. Affidavit of 27 January 1937, quoted in *They Framed Stephenson,* Butler, 140.

11. *Indianapolis News,* 28 November 1927.

12. Niblack, *Hoosier Judge,* 218.

13. *Indianapolis News,* 21 December 1956.

14. *Indianapolis News,* 13 May 1925.

15. *Louisville Courier-Journal,* 17 September 1978.

16. Coughlan, "Konklave in Kokomo," 128.

12. One Klan Dies, Another Rises: The New Klan

1. Niblack, *Hoosier Judge,* 191.

2. Lynd and Lynd, *Middletown,* 122.

3. Klanwatch Project, *Special Report* 3d ed. (Montgomery, Ala.: Southern Poverty Law Center, 1988), 21.

4. The so-called Kentucky and Virginia Resolutions were drafted by Jefferson and Madison in 1798 in opposition to the Alien and Sedition Acts. Under these acts "dangerous" aliens could be summarily deported by the president, and editors critical of Congress or the administration were fined and jailed for malicious writing. The resolutions declared the acts despotic and unconstitutional and asserted the right of individual states to nullify them or interpose their own sovereignty against them. The resolutions passed in the legislatures of both states, but no further state action was taken and the acts expired under Republican opposition.

5. Klanwatch, Southern Poverty Law Center, *Special Report,* 23.

6. Connie Lynch, in *Free at Last,* a history of the civil rights movement, Civil Rights Education Project, (Montgomery Ala.: Southern Poverty Law Center, 1989) 59.

7. Mayor Marion Barry, publicly an opponent of the drug traffic, was charged with possession and use of crack cocaine and perjury before a grand jury. Out of a series of charges, however, a trial jury—apparently feeling he had been the victim of entrapment by law officers—convicted him of only one minor drug possession charge.

8. Rooney was quoted in the Los Angeles magazine the *Advocate* as having said "most people are born with equal intelligence, but blacks have watered down their genes because the less intelligent ones are the ones that have the most children." He denied the quote as reported and called it the work of a "careless reporter." He denied he was a racist and it was recalled that in 1968 he had won an Emmy award for his script for a special show about blacks, "Black History: Lost, Strayed, or Stolen."

9. Klanwatch, *Special Report,* 49.

10. Ibid., 46.

L'Envoi: Onward Christian Soldiers

1. Booth, *Mad Mullah,* 330.

2. Quoted in bulletin from People for the American Way, April 1988.

3. Quoted in *Forum,* publication of People for the American Way, Spring 1990.

4. Couglan, "Konklave in Kokomo," 129.

Works Cited

Bentley, Max. "The Ku Klux Klan in Indiana". *McClure's Magazine,* 58, (May 1924).

Bethen, Francis S., S. J. *The Roman Index of Forbidden Books.* St. Louis, Mo. and London: B. Herder Book Co., 1917.

Bohn, Frank. "The Ku Klux Klan Interpreted." *American Journal of Sociology* 30 (1925): 385–407.

Booth, Edgar Allen. *The Mad Mullah of America.* Columbus, Ohio: Boyd Ellison, 1927.

Busch, Francis X. *Guilty or Not Guilty?* Indianapolis, New York: Bobbs-Merrill Co., 1952.

Butler, Robert A. *So They Framed Stephenson.* Huntington, Indiana: Privately published, 1940.

Chalmers, David M. *Hooded Americanism.* Garden City, New York: Doubleday and Co., 1965.

Commager, Henry Steele. *The American Mind.* New Haven: Yale University Press, 1950.

Coughlan, Robert. "Konklave in Kokomo." In *The Aspirin Age, 1919–1941,* edited by Isabel Leighton, New York: Simon and Schuster, 1949.

Elson, Ruth Miller. *Guardians of Tradition: American Schoolbooks of the Nineteenth Century.* Lincoln, Nebraska: University of Nebraska Press, 1964.

Evansville (Indiana) Courier. 1, 6 May 1920; 27 March, 9, 10 June 1922.

Evans, Hiram Wesley, "The Klan's Fight for Americanism." *North American Review.* March 1926.

———. "The Klan of Tomorrow." Evans pamphlet quoted in *A New History of the United States* by William Miller. New York: George Braziller, 1958.

Free at Last—A History of the Civil Rights Movement. Montgomery, Alabama: The Southern Poverty Law Center, 1989.

Frost, Stanley. *Outlook.* 4 June 1924.

Gilliom, Arthur. *Gilliom's Case Against the Indiana Klan.* Archives of the State of Indiana.

Harrison, Morton. "Gentlemen from Indiana." *Atlantic,* May 1928.

Indianapolis News. 16 January 1924; 12, 13 May 1924; 13 May 1925; 4 June 1925; 7, 8, 14 October 1926; 21 December 1926; 28 November 1927.

Indianapolis Star. 26 May 1924; 5 July 1924.

Indianapolis Times. 4 June 1923; 23, 26 May 1924; 30 October 1924; 15 October 1926; 25 June 1927; 24 February 1927.

Klanwatch Project, *Special Report,* 3d Ed. Montgomery, Alabama: The Southern Poverty Law Center, 1988.

Kokomo (Indiana) Dispatch. 16 November 1925.

Loucks, E. H. *The Ku Klux Klan in Pennsylvania.* Harrisburg, Pennsylvania: Telegraph Press, 1936.

Louisville (Kentucky) Courier-Journal. 17 September 1978.

Lynd, Robert S. and Lynd, Helen M. *Middletown.* New York: Harcourt, Brace and Co., 1929.

Martin, John Bartlow. *Indiana: An Interpretation.* New York: Alfred A. Knopf, 1947.

Mecklin, John Moffatt. *The Ku Klux Klan: A Study of the American Mind.* New York: Harcourt, Brace and Co., 1924.

Mencken, H. L. and Nathan, George Jean, eds. *Smart Set.* February and March 1923.

Monteval, Marion [pseud.] *The Klan Inside Out.* Claremore, Oklahoma. 1924.

Moore, Samuel Taylor. "A Klan Kingdom Collapses." *Independent.* 6 December 1924.

———. "How the Kleagles Collected the Cash." *Independent.* 13 December 1924.

———. "The Consequences of the Klan." *Independent.* 30 December 1924.

Mott, Frank Luther. *A History of American Journalism, 1690–1960.* New York: Macmillan, 1962.

New Catholic Encyclopedia. New York: McGraw-Hill Book Co., 1967.

New York Times. 3 February 1924.

Niblack, John L. *The Life and Times of a Hoosier Judge.* Greenfield, Indiana. 1940.

Works Cited

Noblesville (Indiana) Daily Ledger. 17, 21 November 1925.

People for the American Way. *Bulletin,* April 1988. *Forum,* Spring 1990.

Price, Willadene. *Gutzon Borglum: Artist and Patriot,* 1972 edition.

Randel, William Peirce. *The Ku Klux Klan: A Century of Infamy.* Philadelphia, New York: Chilton Book Co., 1965.

Rice, Arnold S. *The Ku Klux Klan in American Politics.* New York: Haskell House, 1972.

Safianow, Allen. " 'Konklave in Kokomo' Revisited." *Historian* 50:3 (May 1988).

Tait, Samuel. *American Mercury,* (April 1926).

Taylor, Alva. "What the Klan Did in Indiana." *New Republic,* (November 30, 1927).

Weaver, Norman F. "The Knights of the Ku Klux Klan in Wisconsin, Indiana, Ohio, and Michigan." Ph.D. diss. University of Wisconsin, 1954.

Wilson, William E. "Long Hot Summer in Indiana." *American Heritage,* (August 1965).

Index

Index